CONSCIOUSNESS
AND THE
COSMOS

Kabbalah Publishing is a registered DBA of
The Kabbalah Centre International, Inc.

For further information:

The Kabbalah Centre
155 E. 48th St., New York, NY 10017
1062 S. Robertson Blvd., Los Angeles, CA 90035

1.800.Kabbalah www.kabbalah.com

First Edition, February 2013

Formerly published under the title of Star Connection, this
edition is edited and updated with more contemporary
language. Original edition was published in 1986.

Printed in Canada

ISBN: 978-1-57189-874-6

Design: HL Design (Hyun Min Lee) www.hldesignco.com

KABBALIST RAV BERG

CONSCIOUSNESS
AND THE
COSMOS

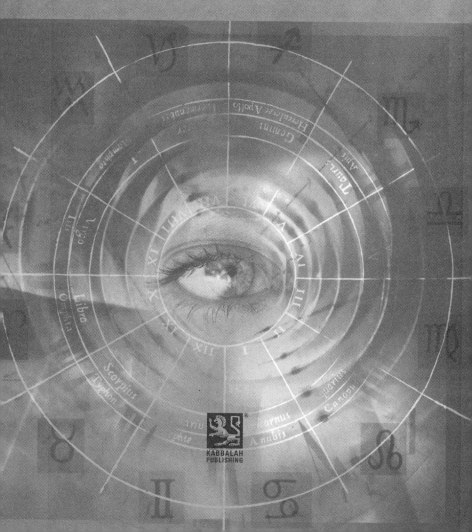

KABBALAH
PUBLISHING

For my wife
Karen
In the vastness of cosmic space
and
the infinity of lifetimes,
it is my bliss to share a soul mate and
an Age of Aquarius with you.

TABLE OF CONTENTS

"THE HEAVENS DECLARE THE GLORY OF THE CREATOR,
THE EXPANSE OF THE SKY TELLS OF HIS HANDIWORK.
DAY FOLLOWING DAY BRINGS EXPRESSION OF PRAISE
AND NIGHT FOLLOWING NIGHT BESPEAKS WISDOM."

—*Psalms* 19:2-3

INTRODUCTION

S ince my entry into the world of mysticism, I have been interested in astrology, sensing that there is more to it than what conventional astrology books provide. What to me seemed most disturbing was the dichotomy between science, astronomy, and Western culture on the one hand, and the esoteric dimension of astrology, with its potential influence upon our universe and the individual, on the other. I was deeply disappointed with the quality of research and science found in the writings of most astrologers.

When widespread disillusionment with the scientific community began to take hold during the early 1970s, one field of scientific endeavor remained untouched: The science of the heavens. Astronomy, with its cosmic soul connection that unquestionably had its origins in the remote past, remains for us today as potent a symbol as ever of the need for a wider explanation of scientific endeavor.

The compulsive fascination with exploration of the unknown out there in our universe has existed within man for as long as he has been able to observe the structure and order of the cosmos. This preoccupation with the cosmic realm and its powerful influence over the affairs of man is firmly established; astronomy has always held a significance for us beyond the simple matter of navigation.

The ancient worship of planetary bodies in the heavens, the mystical astrologer .whose interpretation of cosmic influence and its relationship to man's destiny and future, testify to the ancient past of the science of astronomy. More recent developments in technology and a deluge of information concerning cosmic systems have shown that the universe is far more bewildering and complex than was suspected. It is clear that our understanding of the celestial world beyond the sky is still in its infancy and the exact nature of man and his relationship to our vast universe is as yet only dimly perceived.

Since time immemorial, people have been moved by the unfolding perspective of the universe provided by ancient astronomers and astrologers. Yet with each new discovery, the information gleaned has seemed more confusing and baffling creating more mysteries and questions than clarity and answers. And now, in spite of the enormous and rapid social progress that can be attributed to advanced technology, most people perceive that scientific values threaten their very existence. When some physicists regard the singularity in which a star can collapse without limit until it has shrunk away to an overpowering invisibility as the end of space and time, we are gradually drawing close to the disintegration of the known laws of nature. Considering social as well as scientific implications, we should be searching for the interface between the supernatural and the natural, the bridge between the unknown and the known.

When I was led to the ancient and first known work on Kabbalah, the *Sefer Yetzirah (Book of Formation)*, authored by Abraham the Patriarch, I realized that I had indeed found the missing link: A connection that would provide a vast realm of potential wisdom of astrology in all its deeper ramifications and importance for us today. In this book, I will explain what I found, which is an in-depth study into the fields of extra-terrestrial intelligences, interplanetary relationships, astronomy, and cosmic energy fields that will blow away the skepticism of many people in Western society. In a sense, this book will be a study of the subject of astrology as it was interpreted by a long line of kabbalists in their search for the ultimate meaning of the cosmos and its application to human life on this fleeting terrestrial plane. In this regard, what struck me most as I began my study was the cosmic language of which these kabbalists made use, and more importantly, the methodology that enabled them to use Kabbalah to perceive the essential reality. This understanding provided the kabbalists with answers as to how and why these cosmic intelligences began and about the nature of their internal structures.

All these factors taken together led me to the values and simple truths that have served to remove the veil of occultism that has for too long surrounded the study of astrology.

Einstein said:

> *Pure logical thinking cannot yield us any knowledge of the empirical world; all knowledge of reality starts from experience and ends in it. Propositions arrived at by purely logical means are completely empty as regards reality.*
> —Albert Einstein, *Essays in Science: Ideas and Opinions*

When there is a discovery made beyond the obvious structure as we see it, this invites trouble, as does any attempt to persuade others to perceive things through a lens or perspective other than their own. Who, then, is to determine what is real or unreal concerning our planetary system? And how are they to do it? Most astronomical conclusions are based on the evolutionary theory of the Big Bang, but one must question the validity of these conclusions in their entirety, especially since the primary and essential question of the reason for the Big Bang never has been accurately determined.

From everything we have learned about astrophysics in the past half century, we still do not have answers to some simple questions, the foremost being: What really took place immediately prior to, during, and after the Big Bang?

There is, in fact, only one course that should be pursued: We must return to the moment of the Big Bang for a rendezvous with the cosmic intelligence that was there at the time, which we can do by connecting with those credible kabbalists who made just such a trip and returned from an encounter with the Big Bang by way of mystical time travel. While time travel, according to physicists, is beyond our present capabilities, traveling backward in time has been known for centuries to those steeped in the wisdom of Kabbalah. Please stay with me here, and I will explain.

The traditional notions of space and time, once considered separate and distinct, became inextricably linked by Einstein's theory of relativity. Subsequently, they were recognized by scientists as a fourth dimension of our universe, and this new understanding led to the realization that we can move through time just as we move through space. Relativity has taken us beyond our consciousness and experience, and conventional reasoning seems to have become obsolete.

We are told by scientists that if we could travel faster than the speed of light, time would actually proceed into the past. An astronaut capable, by some means as yet unknown to physical science, of exceeding the speed of light could conceivably travel into deep space and then return home before he left—a thought that at one time could never have been accepted by the scientific community and which was certainly beyond the comprehension of the layman.

When a scientist begins talking about elastic time—time that can be extended or reduced, stretched or shrunk—and places where time no longer exists or where subatomic particles travel back in time, established laws of science have to, of necessity, be reconsidered. Though such an understanding of time may appear to be unacceptable to most of us, it nevertheless opens the doors to even more, and stranger, phenomena and seems to challenge our most rigid laws of logic. While mathematical formulae suggest two-way time travel, the paradoxical consequences keep it within the framework of science fiction for the most part.

The most common flaw in the concept of such two-way time travel is known as the "grandfather paradox." A time traveler would encounter this paradox if he returned to the past just in time to prevent the meeting of his grandparents, which would mean that he himself would never have been born. But had he not been born, he could not have prevented the meeting of his grandparents or be alive to go back in time in the first place. From the world view of the kabbalist, as stated by Rav Ashlag, there is nothing paradoxical about such a trip, simply because the time traveler would prevent the meeting of his grandparents, not in the universe in which he was born but in a parallel universe in which he never existed prior to or after his invasive junket. (*Ten Luminous Emanations*, Volume Two, pgs. 19-21)

This imaginary paradox, however, is little more than a child's puzzle compared with some of the real paradoxes that now confront the physicist. One of which might very well spell the breakdown of our presently conceived laws of nature or even the end of the world for science. It is the discovery, in mathematical terms at least, of space-time naked singularities or black holes, which come about as a result of the gravitational collapse of giant stars. Black holes hold bizarre properties. Absolutely nothing, not even light, can escape their immense gravity. Even the original intelligence that produced the black hole in the first place is trapped within it. It is precisely at this point that the gaps in our understanding of the workings of the physical universe have arisen. The image of our physical universe is one of a complex web of influences, closely interwoven, continually acting and reacting among its integral parts.

Inasmuch as man is internally fragmented, so, too, only a fragment of the total picture can be understood. Yet it is commonly accepted that everything that happens in our universe is entirely dependent upon and determined by everything else. Along with the threat of naked singularities, our frail minds must face the chaos of our universe. Many scientists today believe that the entire cosmos is slowly disintegrating, just as are the organized structures we call our bodies. Just as people grow old and die, and mountains are washed away, the ultimate stage of stellar depletion of energy is the black hole with which nothing survives an encounter. When an object falls into a black hole, all form, intelligence, and identity are wiped out forever. This rather depressing conclusion about the inevitability of entropy has led many scientists to assume that the entire universe will eventually become nothing more than a burned-out cosmic cinder.

What, then, is the purpose of the celestial bodies? How and why did they come into being? Without some answers to these fundamental questions, we can never face up to the ultimate unknowable future. We must take our chances on whatever the universe throws at us. Any attempt—and there have been many attempts by science in the past 300 years—

to explain and describe the enormous and beautifully designed universe we now inhabit with information based upon events that occurred after the Big Bang leaves all conclusions hanging by a thread. Physicists still cling to the belief that understanding our cosmos lies not in its origin, structure, and organization, but rather in the understanding of the laws and principles of nature that maintain the cosmic system and force it to operate in an orderly fashion. To ignore the purpose behind each cause and effect simply because this issue is very complex and subtle appears to be a cheap way out for physics. Probability, which still plays a large part in subatomic physics, has failed to explain adequately the physics that lie beyond gravitational collapse. Indeed, such uncertainty well might spell the end of the road for physics as an exact science. I am sure that as we probe nature more deeply, we will enter a new era in physics—one more basic and more beautiful. This seems to be the expectation of John Wheeler, the famous astrophysicist, who in his book *The Physicists' Conception of Nature* wrote: "Someday, a door will surely open and expose the glittering central mechanism of the world in its beauty and simplicity. Toward the arrival of that day, no development holds out more hope than the paradox of gravitational collapse."

The path to this new age of physics, which lies beyond the boundaries of infinity where the limitations of light speed cease to exist, is provided by the *Zohar* (*Book of Splendor*). Rav Shimon bar Yochai, the author of the *Zohar*, stated that in order to face the unknowable, it is necessary to discover the cause of these events, an undertaking that presents a challenge that contemporary physics cannot deal with. It is precisely this encounter with the unknowable that a few scientists have declared will remain forever beyond the domain of intellectual inquiry. Yet ancient kabbalists held the key, as the following passage from the *Zohar*[1] indicates:

> *Rav Elazar and Rav Aba were sitting together one evening, and when it grew dusk, they went to a garden by the Sea of Kinneret. As they were going, they saw two stars rush towards each other from different points in the sky, meet, and then disappear. Said Rav Aba, "How mighty are the works of the Creator, the Primordial Cause, both in Heaven above and in the Earth below! Who can understand it, these two stars emerging from different directions, then meeting and disappearing?" Rav Elazar replied, "Did we not see them? For we reflected upon them as on many other great works that the Creator is constantly performing."*

While a complete description of stars in general and their function in particular is beyond the scope of this introduction, several points within this very abstruse *Zohar* passage are worth noting.

From a kabbalistic view, there are principally two types of stars and their internal intelligence structure resembles the electron. The basic property of stars, their mass or energy charge originates from and consists of one of three primary forces of negative intelligence, including male and female negative energy forces. Stars themselves act as an extension of these energy charges. A star that makes manifest the female negative energy force is drawn from the southern cosmic energy field referred to as the Right, or positive, Column. A star that manifests the male negative energy force draws its internal intelligence from the northern cosmic energy field referred to as the Left, or negative, Column.

This is the explanation for the cosmic meeting of the two celestial bodies in the *Zohar* passage above. One structure was of a male negative intelligence and the other was a female negative intelligence force. When they were drawn to each other, they nullified one another, shrinking and returning to their unmanifested state of pure undifferentiated intelligence waiting to become manifest again. Their return to their original state is accomplished through time travel exceeding the speed of light and running off again to infinity waiting for their intelligence to make its next move. This scenario, expressed in metaphysical rather than physical terms, sounds as if it is taken from a science fiction drama; nonetheless, we have been provided with this account by two noted kabbalists for whom time travel to the past did not appear to be a problem. The reply of Rav Elazar, "Did we not see them? For we reflected upon them as on many other great works," indicates that they could recognize and qualify the internal structure of these celestial bodies. For these sages, facing the infinite did not prove to be a harrowing experience; nor, for that matter, did facing a universe that abounds with infinity.

Another point worth noting is that in nature there is no inherent unpredictability that becomes manifest. Nor should energy forces be envisaged as roaming around in a random sort of way. It is our inability to define and recognize the various energy-intelligences at their subatomic or celestial level that keeps us from defining concepts. Rav Elazar, who achieved an elevated state of consciousness, found no difficulty in defining precisely what was taking place. He could tap into information that made both the future and the past clear realities. Assuming we are ready for the new age of infinity, how does one go about gathering this kind of information?

The author of the *Zohar*[2] envisaged this epoch-making Aquarian period by providing some of the knowledge that now has become necessary:

> *For there is not a concept or aspect within the human body that does not have its counterpart in the world as a whole. For a man's body consists of varying degrees of concepts and aspects, all acting and reacting upon each other so as to form one organism. So does the world at large consist of a hierarchy of created things that, when they properly act and react upon each other, together form literally one organic body?*

What seems to emerge from the *Zohar* is a phenomenon best described as parallel and interrelated yet independent universes. These universes are composed of an endless number of tracks that reflect different patterns and outcomes for each of the lives of an individual. We might crudely compare this phenomenal concept with our present-day computer systems, which include varied programs within one piece of hardware.

Our frames of reference concerning the speed-of-light barrier deal more specifically with the physical world as we see it. Reality, as observed by the kabbalist, is composed of infinite metaphysical references where time or the speed-of-light barrier cease to exist. Synchronous events have been reduced by the scientific community to "mere coincidence" if they come into conflict with the limiting concept of the light-speed barrier, yet according to Einstein's theory of relativity, any influence between particles must require an energy transfer although this energy cannot move instantaneously. Energy can move only at the speed of light or less. The *Zohar*[3] suggests that the quantum physics theory is correct, but it also states[4] that there is a never-ending contact that continues to influence other events, no matter how far apart they seem to be from each other. According to the *Zohar*, communication can take place instantaneously across the universe. When we fail to observe this phenomenon, the inability lies within the vessel's limited capability to reveal it. The instant contact, which exceeds the speed of light, has already taken place.

From a kabbalistic viewpoint, matters of metaphysics should and can be validated. Recall the urging of Rav Shimon bar Yochai that the concepts of metaphysics be considered on the basis that such concepts could, in some form, be validated by manifestations and physical expressions.

From the wisdom of Kabbalah set out for us by kabbalistic masters, we can gain an insight into the whys of the entire spectrum of astronomy that the scientist is still unable to penetrate. Kabbalistic astrology, in penetrating this celestial inner sanctum, provides plausible explanations for the movements of solar activity, thus allowing us to take a giant step forward in bridging the gap and providing the necessary link between celestial and terrestrial entities.

How do we really know, from a biblical viewpoint, that astral influences do exist? Several parts of the Bible, once decoded, provide the answer, starting with:

> *And God made two great lights: The greater light to rule the day and the lesser light to rule the night. He made the stars also to rule over the day and night and to divide the light from the darkness. And the evening and morning were the fourth day.* (*Genesis* 1:16-19)

Just how involved is the Bible with the heavenly bodies? It is no exaggeration to say that the Bible is freighted with material dealing with the Heavens. By the words "to rule," the Bible means "to manifest or to dominate." The sun and the moon, specifically referred to in the foregoing verse, are cited as "ruling" bodies. So from this biblical verse from the days of Creation, we are given our first biblical support for astrology as a discipline of importance. The seven days of Creation, from a *Zoharic* standpoint, are specifically related to the seven planets of astrology as "rulers" of our galaxy.

The beauty of why there are seven planets in the discipline of astrology, rather than eight or nine, will be more fully discussed in a later chapter.

Another indication of the importance of astral influences and their composition is revealed in the *Zohar* and *Sefer Yetzirah* (*Book of Formation*), concerning what might appear to be a very unimportant part of the Bible, namely, Jacob and his 12 sons. (*Genesis* 29:32-35, *Genesis* 30) The *Zohar* asks what importance the Bible assigns to the fact that Jacob had 12 sons, rather than 11 or 13. Those who compiled the Bible considered astrology to be the hand of the Creator written boldly across the Heavens. It is natural for the Bible to reveal spiritual or metaphysical rulership (note again the words "to rule") by matching the 12 sons of Jacob to their corresponding 12 constellations.

The Bible goes into great detail to elaborate how the names of each of the 12 sons were chosen. In effect, from a kabbalistic viewpoint, this reflects the astrology of the Bible by having each son of Jacob assigned spiritual or metaphysical rulership over his particular constellation. The story of Jacob and his 12 sons is the genesis of the Jewish people and it evolved accordingly. Those who believe the study of astrology to be foreign to Judaism must therefore reconcile their belief with this elaborate biblical tale that goes to great lengths in describing the birth of each of the 12 sons of Jacob as well as the rationale behind each son's name. If this information were not of supreme importance, it does not seem conceivable that the Bible would devote such a great amount of ink to the story.

TRIBE	SEFIRA	MONTH	SIGN (Hebrew)	SIGN (English)	ZODIAC (Conventional)
Reuben	Chesed	Nissan	Taleh	Lamb	Aries
Shimon	Gevurah	Iyar	Shor	Ox	Taurus
Levi	Tiferet	Sivan	Te'omim	Twins	Gemini
Yehuda	Netzach	Tammuz	Sartan	Crab	Cancer
Issaschar	Hod	Av	Aryeh	Lion	Leo
Zebulon	Yesod	Elul	Betulah	Virgin	Virgo
Benjamin	Chesed	Tishrei	Moznaim	Scales	Libra
Dan	Gevurah	Mar-	Akrav	Scorpion	Scorpio
Naphtali	Tiferet	Cheshvan	Keshet	Rainbow	Sagittarius
Gad	Netzach	Kislev	G'di	Goat	Capricorn
Asher	Hod	Tevet	D'li	Vessel	Aquarius
Joseph	Yesod	Shevat	Dagim	Fishes	Pisces
		Adar			

Another important reference for which the *Zohar* has an extensive interpretation is *Numbers* 2:1-29, which says:

> *Every man of the children of Israel shall pitch by his own standard with the ensign of his father's house.... And on the east side toward the rising of the sun shall they of the standard of the camp of Judah pitch their armies... and those that pitch next to him shall be the tribe of Issachar... then the tribe of Zebulun.*

The passage continues:

> ... *On the south side shall be the standard of the camp*
> *of Reuben, according to their armies.... And those who*
> *pitch by him shall be the tribe of Simeon... then the*
> *tribe of Gad (2:10)... On the west side shall be the*
> *standard of the camp of Ephraim (2:18)... and by him*
> *shall be the tribe of Manasseh (2:20)... then the tribe*
> *of Benjamin (2:22)....*
>
> *The standard of the camp of Dan shall be on the north*
> *side (2:25), and those that encamp by him shall be the*
> *tribe of Asher (2:27)... then the tribe of Naphtali....*
> *(2:29)*

Thus, we have three tribes on the east side, three on the south side, and three on the west corresponding to Right, Left and Central columns, and representing the original elements of earth, air, fire, and water. Each tribe understood the power of the cosmos, and their flags became—and controlled—the 12 signs of the zodiac.

This seemingly abstruse passage actually describes the body of knowledge that is the totality of astrology. It is one of many coded passages in the Bible, and it means simply that by the power of God, given to the Israelites in the Great *Exodus*, people from that day forward would have control over their own lives, should they desire to exercise it.

The key word here is "sign," and it corresponds to the verse in Genesis 1:14:

> *Let there be lights in the firmament of the Heavens to divide the day from the night, and let them be for signs and for seasons, and for days and years.*

The word "sign" is a reference to the signs of the zodiac—Jacob's sons—which were potentially created on the fourth day along with all of the other planets.

From such a seed, planted at one and the same time in the wilderness of Sinai and in the Heavens above it, did the kabbalistic view of astrology grow. Let us therefore examine it—root, trunk, branch, and leaf—and learn how it holds far more than the traits and alleged fortunes of sun signs offered in daily newspapers.

*"A FOOL SEES NOT THE SAME TREE AS
A WISE MAN SEES."*

—William Blake, *A Memorable Fancy*

CHAPTER ONE

A SEARCH FOR CREDENTIALS

One of the principal arguments against astral influences is based on the assumption that the "science" of astrology is either completely unknown or is totally incredible. The usual question is: How can planets possibly influence our day-to-day affairs on this earth? Examine this question closely and you will see that it is based on the premise that a causal relationship cannot exist between objects separated by distance and not physically or otherwise linked. It is like saying that what the eye does not see and what the ear does not hear simply does not exist. However, this could be a valid argument either in support of or in opposition to astrology. In astrology, what one accepts or does not accept is an important matter. The other sciences can be verified by experiment and consequently are subject to the workings of the laws and principles of science. Astrology has developed from pure metaphysics and cannot be verified the same way as a physical science.

A physicist, to make the point even stronger, will say that the universe is composed of a vast number of particles of matter in electromagnetic fields, and any events or changes that may take place result from the impact of one force (or particle) upon another. It is this notion of causality—that one particle has caused another to move—that the whole framework of science, as we know it today, is based on. In astrology, however, this causal relationship between two objects is separated by immense gulfs of empty space not unlike that which stretches between the Earth and the moon.

Experts love to classify astrology as an unscientific system somewhere between a pastime and the occult, superstition, and mysticism. Its sister science, astronomy, was recognized as a real science only after Copernicus proved that the Earth, far from being the center of the universe, was merely one tiny part of a single solar system. Through telescopic astronomy, it was revealed that the individual members of the solar system obeyed mysterious but exact laws and principles.

Astrology, on the other hand, cannot meet this test of proof. The most that one might expect in the validation of astrology is that there seems to be some evidence that it works. The question of why it works, up until the publication of this book, has not been addressed. But even in other disciplines, there is no physicist or scientist who can explain why things work the way they do. Physics is called physics because it basically attempts to explain *what is*, rather than provide some plausible explanation of *why it is*.

This book will attempt to validate the study of astrology by explaining the *why* of solar and lunar activity, planetary motion, and seasonal shifts by examining the effect they have upon those who live under their influence.

The composition and structure of planetary forces have eluded all of our space explorations. The surface of celestial bodies and their gravitational and magnetic fields are of a nature that defies direct investigation by even the most advanced spacecraft. Science, therefore, is able to provide us with very little in the way of definitive information. Man landed on the moon and returned with samples of the rocks that litter its surface but none of this activity has provided us with the overall answers that we seek. Man has one very serious handicap: He cannot always see what he is looking at, especially on the surface of the moon. The moon is an entirely different frame of reference for our limited minds; we are insulated from it by a spacesuit, boots, and a canned and compressed earth atmosphere. Even the data we relay back to Earth by telemetry is subject to a host of unknown forces that can distort meaning.

Indeed, we have enough trouble observing our environment right here on our own familiar terrestrial level, Earth, where we were born and bred. We have difficulty really seeing things that we look at. We have come to trust our five senses, and along came Werner Heisenberg to tell us that we must apply the uncertainty principle to everything because the things with which we come into direct contact present so many problems that we stand on the brink of no reality! There are no absolutes.

Nature continues to draw a curtain across its face whenever scientists attempt to obtain information that seems inconsistent with quantum mechanics. Heisenberg's injection of the uncertainty principle rules out the possibility of anyone ever being able to perform the measurements needed to define any physical idea, leaving us with no precise definition of the real or even the unreal. Philosophers have struggled with this problem for years but only recently, have we begun to hear about it from the physicists who are in a greater dilemma because the more that technology advances, the further they are taken from reality.

What one does not "know" is that which one has not come into contact with. "Adam knew Eve, and she conceived and bore Cain." (*Genesis* 4:1) How can the mere act of "knowing" create a pregnancy? The *Zohar* explains this idea simply as the difference between information and knowing: Knowing is the connection. Obviously, there was an act of physical intercourse, but that is not the point sought by the *Zohar*, which cites this particular verse in Genesis to illustrate that information only becomes knowledge when direct contact has been made with the information sought. Only the experience of something, as opposed to the mere awareness that something exists, even on a metaphysical level, yields to knowing. Therefore, since man, still imprisoned in his other frames of reference including space suits and a canned atmosphere, never actually "touched" the moon, we cannot really know it even though the information sent back to Earth via telemetry may fill volumes.

There is no such thing as an unrelated, completely independent entity in this universe. Consequently, the accuracy of anything received on Earth from a space probe must be questioned, as it can be distorted under the new theory of quantum physics or, for that matter, under metaphysical influences originating from other areas of the cosmos.

Any maker of microchips will be able to explain the challenge that quantum mechanics imposes upon the process of locating a single electron using an electron microscope. The microscope uses a stream of electrons to take the target electron's measurements, but by the time the sought electron is "found," the electron stream used in the probe has moved it so that it isn't there anymore. The very act of observation changes that which is being observed, forcing microchip makers to play blind statistical odds in the creation of their tiny miracles.

These observation problems, moreover, exist on the macrocosmic as well as the microcosmic, plane. Astronomers initially thought that Saturn boasted only six rings, but telemetry received from recent robot probes has indicated that there are more than one thousand and that what may appear to be no more than haphazard "noise" within those rings may be more closely related to intelligence. No matter how closely we monitor intelligence, by the time we connect with it, it has already undergone enormous changes because of the principles of quantum mechanics. Thus, any conclusions arrived at—what we would consider "knowledge" of the phenomenon—must, of necessity, include uncertainty. What, then, is real? Using his very limited base of knowledge and refusing to come to grips with what actually *has* become reality, the poor physicist stumbles on whatever it may have been when he first went searching for it. How does he reconcile his work with Einstein's theories, inasmuch as it was within Einstein's frame of reference that energy could move only at the speed of light or less? What is of influence on the physical level or, even more importantly, at the mental level where synchronous events take place seemingly with no mutual connection?

According to the *Zohar*, quantum physics does not operate only on the physical plane. The *Zohar* states that "man is an exact replica of the universe as a whole," meaning that events occurring within the human body are doing so with energy transfers far greater than the speed of light.

From a kabbalistic point of view, light has no speed whatsoever. To the kabbalist, light is ever-present and pervades the universe, even though we lack the ability to see it.

When an object, or vessel, such as a light bulb actually reveals light for us it was there in the first place, we erroneously conclude that the light we see has come into existence only with the throwing of a switch. Thus, when we observe movement, or speed, we are really only considering the action of the vessel that reveals the light, not the light itself.

The kabbalist, on the other hand, views the light as well as the vessels that contain and reveal it. The vessels exist on many levels, and as we delve further into the subatomic realms, we will reach levels where reactions will be well in excess of the scientist's view of the speed of light. Once that fallacious speed of light has been exceeded, two-way time travel—into the past or into the future—can occur. Thus, we can relate to the hymn that refers to God, which states that "He was, He is, and He will be," all at the same time. From a kabbalistic perspective, "He"—God—is an all-inclusive positive energy and Light of Wisdom. What the verse means is that the essence of Light is universal and its presence is found simultaneously, instantaneously, and beyond any aspect of time.

For all his brilliance, Einstein, steadfastly clinging to his speed-of-light theory, failed to come to terms with the many contradictions that point to the fact that on another level, there is no such thing as a light-speed barrier.

Knowledge is not measured as physical energy. When we speak of knowledge, we speak of knowing, which is consciousness. As abstract as this term may seem, consciousness is simply a physical cable by which energy is transferred, and is not limited to the speed of light. Consciousness is to light speed what the atomic world of Einstein is to the subatomic world of the future where different frames of reference, different rules, different laws, and different principles must be used. From Newton to Einstein, we have come to the world of crystals, then molecules, then atoms, but the field of science does not stop there. From the atom, we have proceeded to subatomic particles and now find ourselves at the threshold of true reality, which is consciousness existing far beyond the pitiful five or ten percent possessed by the average individual. With the revelation of each new level of reality from the mechanical to the conscious, each level will behave according to precise laws and principles no more contradictory than Einstein's physics is to Newton's.

Those laws and principles have room for many phenomena deemed fantasy by most laymen and by virtually all scientists: Paranormal abilities, including ESP (extrasensory perception), precognition and telekinesis; parallel universes; and the metaphysical DNA of the soul. All these phenomena exist in one frame of reference or another, yet surprisingly enough, they are rejected out of hand by people who have no trouble whatsoever accepting the fact that an astronaut aboard a space capsule can circumnavigate the globe in an hour at speeds unattainable within the atmosphere, simply because he does so in the altered frame of reference of space.

This simple example leads us into an area where different frames of reference, different universal tracks, and consequently, different laws and principles of logic are found: The area of parallel worlds or universes.

The principles of DNA may be used to illustrate the point as it applies to the soul. By DNA, I mean here the metaphysical DNA or the reincarnation of DNA levels from a previous lifetime, which determines the physical DNA level as we know it in this lifetime. This leap, however, takes us below the quantum level, to the sub-quantum world of hidden variables. It is the physical world that causes the phenomena we observe on this worldly level, but it is really from the underlying spaceless, timeless realm that events of ordinary reality emerge. The growing convergence of data from different sources already suggests the plurality of levels, both on our own physical plane and at the sub-quantum level. We are beginning to probe deeper for these myriad levels of intelligent life forms.

At this level, the mind cannot physically express more than one dimension at a time. It is in the sub-quantum area—in kabbalistic terminology, in the soul—that we find differing but parallel interrelated worlds and universes, each composed of endless universe tracks also called soul-tracks. These soul-tracks are ultimately expressed as different patterns and outcomes for the same person, depending upon the particular level of soul that emerges at any given time.

Different levels, layers, and parallel tracks do not necessarily indicate different realities. How many of us behave a certain way on Monday, then another way on Tuesday? Are we physically two different people? Certainly not. All the divergent entities are part of the one reality that is the all-embracing unity. Everything depends upon the particular soul-track upon which the individual finds himself a passenger at any given time, and different tracks travelled will produce different results.

An important aspect of parallel tracks is the all-embracing seed. Of necessity, the seed must contain all the ultimate physical expressions—from root to the ultimate and final destination, which is the fruit. At the seed level, the varied potential tracks all exist as one unified central force, part of the all-embracing unity concept. The parallel tracks that exist in our universe, will determine the ultimate outcome for the individual, depending on which of them the person takes.

We have already established through the *Zohar* that there are different layers that interact within the human body. So, too, are there different layers in the universe that act and react upon other layers. Outcomes depend upon which particular state is being used—a concept that can be expanded and used in consideration of the soul. Rav Isaac Luria expanded upon this point of parallel levels and universes in his volume *Gates of Reincarnation,* declaring that within each individual soul are three different levels: Soul (*Neshamah*), Spirit (*Ruach*), and Crude Spirit (*Nefesh*), and moreover, that there are metaphysical transfers between levels, or wavelengths, which are channels in which a transfer of energy takes place.

When we speak about a transfer of energy, however, we are not referring to the energy itself, but rather to the revealment of that energy that comes through a vessel. When activated energy is revealed, we observe what we think are streams of energy. But what we are really seeing is the energy that is revealed to us by the activity taking place in the vessel. Thus, when we refer to "speed," we are speaking in terms of the channels and the vessels that reveal the essence of the light. The ultimate is a level where we would not be dealing with light speed, simply because there is no speed of light to discuss. This concept completely negates the principle of Einstein's theory of the speed of light, and it also obviates his fear that surpassing the speed of light would produce so many paradoxes. Yet the possibility of time travel exists within the matrix. Since Einstein could not understand how to address the paradoxes that seemed to arise, he ruled out the possibility that there could be universes where light speed does not exist. But we are beginning to approach just such a place—a place where space-time, as posited by scientists, no longer holds sway and where past, present, and future exist simultaneously.

In kabbalistic terms, light is prevalent and all-pervading. There is no space in this or any other universe that is empty of light, just as at our physical level, there is no space empty of atoms. The parallel is simply that there are two kinds of atomic structures: The mass, or object, in which atoms have joined to become molecules of what appears to be solid matter, and the disjointed state that our hand might pass through with no sensation whatsoever. There may be more atoms in a cubic inch of air than in a cubic inch of table, but in the air, they are unrevealed. Just as the table is the vessel that reveals the atom, the light also needs a vessel to reveal it. This gives rise to a wonderful paradox: Nothing can become revealed unless it first is concealed. We can relate this to our social norms: A person does not reveal himself in a public setting without first being concealed in clothing.

When we delve into the inner essence of things, many layers of revealment are encountered. Among other states of vessels, there is the vessel of the table, measured in time and space. Then there is the vessel of the atom, invisible to the naked eye, but revealed under a microscope. As we probe deeper and deeper, we will find other states revealed—states we consider as consciousness. The table is a state of consciousness. Scientists today have developed a theory matching something long known in Kabbalah: The desire to receive—what kabbalists refer to as the vessel—is an intelligence. Rav Ashlag said that there is a state of consciousness called "table," another called "rock," and still another called "tree." And there is a state of consciousness called "man." All are different, yet all are states, or forms, of consciousness. (*An Entrance to the Zohar*)

Eugene Wigner, a Nobel Prize-winning physicist, wrote of the unreasonable effectiveness of mathematics in the natural sciences in an essay titled "Two Kinds of Reality." "The first," he said, "is my own consciousness, and the second, everything else." Scientific knowledge leans on, and is impossible without, the type of knowledge we acquired as infants. Scientific knowledge is an infinitesimal fraction of the natural knowledge.

Heisenberg wrote of this:

> One might say that the human ability to understand may be, in a certain sense, unlimited. But the existing scientific concepts cover always only a very limited part of reality, and the other part that has not yet been understood is infinite. Whenever we proceed from the known into the unknown, we may hope to understand, but we may have to learn at the same time a new meaning for the word "understanding."

The understanding is recognized even before it is rationally understood in detail. (*Physics and Philosophy,* pg. 200)

When Rav Ashlag referred in 1919 to positive-, negative- and central-column concepts as desires, few appreciated how stunningly remarkable his view of reality was. Little did the world of physics then realize how this theory of intelligence, or consciousness of all matter, would bring us closer to the secret of our universe. Everything was, and is, thought. In *The Mysterious Universe*, famed astrophysicist Sir James Jean wrote: "The universe can be best pictured, although still very imperfectly and inadequately, as consisting of pure thought, the thought of what, for want of a wider word, we must describe as a mathematical thinker."

Rav Ashlag summed up thought in a word: Desire. He said the power of mind and thought move through innumerable channels consisting mainly of a Desire to Receive, Share, and Restrict. This, perhaps, is what Niels Bohr (Einstein's challenger in the quantum theory debate and recipient of the Nobel Prize in physics in 1922, a year after Einstein became a laureate) meant when he [Bohr] told his own son, "You are not thinking; you are merely logical."

Bohr might not have recognized the profundity of his own statement. He was, in fact, stating that when one is connected to the inner space of thought, he is transcending the five percent limiting realm of logic and reaching the understanding that exists long before it is rationally understood. According to Rav Ashlag, this is the achievement of *devekut* or communion with the Original Thought and its thought process.

From a kabbalistic viewpoint, we have the language to discuss different states of consciousness, different levels, different kinds of vessels, different kinds of desires to receive, different kinds of intelligence, and different levels of consciousness. There is only one kind of energy from a kabbalistic viewpoint: The Light of Wisdom. It is the same, no matter where it appears. The only thing that affects it is the nature of the vessel, or kind of consciousness, that receives it. Some kinds of consciousness reveal more Light, others less. Different states of consciousness, different levels, different desires to receive all affect how much or how little Light one perceives.

Ten years ago, the telephone system consisted of heavy cables that could send only a few messages at one time. A microchip now accomplishes the same task and with a greater volume. The amount of electricity that enters any given home is the same. The difference is in the vessel, be it a power-devouring air conditioner, a 15-watt bulb, or a 200-watt bulb. Such vessels, having different degrees of consciousness, determine the amount of energy they will reveal by means of their own concealment.

The meaning of technological advancement is the removal of the physicality of a vessel, gradually bringing it closer to the point at which, in apparent paradox, it would appear that the less the physical material, the more potent the energy flow; in other words, that as the vessel becomes smaller, the amount of energy passing through it increases.

As technology gradually approaches different levels of receiving and varying states of consciousness, it approaches, for all practical purposes, the speed of light and beyond. The tiny microchip now moves more messages at a far quicker pace than did its clumsy predecessor, the cable. It has less physical material, but its level of consciousness is far greater, not only in volume and density but in speed as well. Computers move enormous amounts of information at a time, and as the vessel becomes smaller, it leads us inexorably toward the day when we will use hairline channels and living channels constructed of proteins. And when the channels themselves become living organisms, the speed of light will be surpassed.

The transition is coming more swiftly than any scientist currently imagines, and it heralds a universe in which we will become accustomed to matter as energy itself. Only then will science realize that we are not speaking of the speed of light, but about the speed of vessels.

When a person attains an altered state of consciousness, he can be very material, but his physicality will begin to fade as he moves toward a microchip state of consciousness. With this in mind, the computer has put man into the back seat where his power lies in less, not more, physicality. Much today is written about the use of computers in war to foil the computers of an enemy and to jam his radar by sending counter-signals on the same frequency. But it does not stop with this initial engagement. The enemy radar gets a bit "smarter," with its computers programmed to jump from frequency to frequency, thus avoiding the interference. Our equipment then can be programmed to track the shifting signals and automatically adjust to jam them again in an endless, expensive, and counterproductive cycle. Computer systems locked in such a contest become dangerously obsolete in moments, yet billions of dollars will be spent on such systems simply to build our belief that we are not vulnerable. The futility of such an approach is painfully obvious, but the business of jumping from frequency to frequency is nothing new. Kabbalistic meditation does the same thing with frequencies that exist as parallel levels of the universe. Kabbalistic meditation, however, is designed to reveal the pervading internal Light of Wisdom, the only energy force that is all-pervading as the opposite of the force that is the Desire to Receive.

"ENOUGH OF SCIENCE AND OF ART:
CLOSE UP THESE BARREN LEAVES.
COME FORTH AND BRING WITH YOU
A HEART THAT WATCHES AND RECEIVES."

—William Wadsworth, *The Table Turned*

CHAPTER TWO

DESIRE:
A KEY TO THE COSMOS

The Desire to Receive is central to everything in the cosmos. No form, from a stone to a human being, can exist without it, but it comes in many layers. The more sophisticated forms purify its denser attributes, and the less corporeal it becomes, the more capable it is of transferring or communicating with energy. Remember, there is no such thing as an actual transfer of observed energy.

Wherever speed of light or transfer of energy occurs, vessels are merely revealing the Light of Wisdom, which is all-pervading and does not change. From the kabbalistic viewpoint, there is a transfer of energy through a series of entities that behave like different parts of a cable. When a system is devised, it stretches the concept of the Desire to Receive, extending it just as the cable does. Each time a part of the system is activated there is no transfer of energy, as is commonly accepted in physics, but rather a revealing of the energy that is already there. Although there is no transfer of energy, there appears to be.

When I refer to a system, I specifically refer to the vessels, such as the atoms in the universe that reveal the all-pervading energy that always has existed in an unrevealed state. Our reference to systems, then different systems, then more effective systems, then computer-jamming systems refers to the different levels of vessels that take the Desire to Receive deeper and deeper, down to the point at which they touch the root. This is the difference in intelligence. But what makes up the difference in intelligence at this point that is unseen? What causes differences at this point, and what makes the differences between one system and another?

Intelligence has been defined as different forms of the Desire to Receive, but that is not the root of the matter. To arrive at the root where it all begins, we must delve into sub-atomics where different levels of vessels, now unseen, consist of different gradations of the Desire to Receive, which is the root of intelligence. What accounts for the difference between one intelligence that reveals the all-pervading energy force, and another? The grade of revealment of the Light of Wisdom will be determined where the Desire to Receive has been transmuted into a Desire to Impart and depends upon the degree to which the Desire to Receive has been transmuted. Different, or altered, states of consciousness are different levels of spirituality, and the altering of the Desire to Receive for Oneself Alone to a Desire to Impart is an altering of the level of spirituality.

The purer the internal energy of the vessel is, the greater its intelligence. The revealment in this system is copious because an entire system with an infinite number of segments is involved. When we activate the infinite number of entities that comprise the system, the speed of which has appeared to scientists as the speed of light, only the purest Desire to Receive is brought into play.

As Rav Shimon bar Yochai put it, for us to understand the inner machinations and workings of the metaphysical area, which for all practical purposes remains concealed, we must resort to finding its manifest state on a physical level. Once we find what we consider to be the branch of the root, we will be able to pinpoint the metaphysical aspect of the subject under discussion, which are the different gradations of the Desire to Receive.

Gravity, from a kabbalistic view, is the interior aspect of the Desire to Receive. As we go "up the ladder" and move out of the magnetic field of gravity, we experience another kind of field where gravity ceases to exist. There the coarseness, the density of the impurities that the Desire to Receive inevitably contains, also ceases to exist. Where gravity declines, purity rises in degree.

Getting back to the innermost energy factor that exists in systems, vessels, channels, or cables, where the greatest Desire to Receive exists, so does the greatest lack of speed, but the least Desire to Receive is not the most pure.

Purity is the ability to "transmute" the intense Desire to Receive for Oneself Alone to one of a Desire to Impart that which is received. Friction prevents speed and revealment of the Light of Wisdom. The system is not pure. The purer the system becomes in dealing with proteins and other living organisms, the more gradations there will be to the point of infinity.

The ultimate intelligence is the Endless World, where the Desire to Receive is as pure as the Desire to Impart, but this will never be achieved at our level of life on earth. We would need to go beyond the aspect of space-time, established by Einstein as 186,000 miles per second. The proposition that we cannot achieve this is a complete fallacy that should be done away with as quickly as possible. It does not serve us properly on our level, let alone upon levels sought through different states of consciousness where time and space no longer are factors. Quantum and relativity theories theoretically have established that there is no space-time, but only when we at last understand that intelligence, or consciousness, is in a very pure state can we experience a lessening of the space-time influence.

Altered states of consciousness, from a kabbalistic view, occur when an individual achieves the different levels of the Desire to Receive, which are the different levels of consciousness.

When television networks broadcast on their own frequencies (which are their own particular systems of the overall Desire to Receive), we are inclined to accept the notion that the information being transmitted from the broadcasting station originates there. From a kabbalistic point of view, however, the information has always existed, but in potential form and merely awaiting the channel or revealing instrument that ultimately will make it manifest. Information is an integral part of the all-pervading Light of Wisdom, which includes all information that was, is, and will be. Channels, cables, and systems all are part of the intelligence or Desire to Receive, which itself is the vessel that reveals the information that already exists. Higher or lower frequencies and jamming are all different variations of the revealing system. Only here on Earth can we experience change, otherwise known as the advance of technology. Information, therefore, is only energy that needs to be revealed.

To have the power of precognition, teleportation, or the ability to transfer energy from one person to another involves simply stretching one's own system. How far it will stretch and where it can be directed depends upon the individual system. If we have a total frequency that can pervade the Earth, we will instantly reveal energy that exists throughout the world. The longer the frequency in terms of revealment and distance, the more power it possesses. Voice of America (VOA) pervades the Earth because its creators devised a Desire to Receive system designed for such widespread play. Information and energy are the same thing in the VOA system, just as they are in all systems.

Extrasensory perception, known as ESP, is nothing more than a connection made with another person; it is no more mysterious than a telephone call, although prior to the invention of that instrument, the concept of a telephone was most mysterious indeed. To practice ESP, one must engulf the person he is trying to contact into his own system, but this is possible only by means of a Desire to 'in its pure, unadulterated state in which a balance of a genuine Desire to Impart is included. This process, however, also poses a dark side, which is addressed in the Bible by the concept of Armageddon. (*Ezekiel* 38:1-23) In the Armageddon to come, enemies, for example, who may have attached a high priority to research into the matter, could conceptually engulf us, instantly tapping into any information at hand from those who, having neither knowledge of nor belief in such forces, would have no defense against. The connection is made via the frequency that instantaneously reveals, meaning closest to the Light of Wisdom and its Desire to Share, but the Desire to Receive is a powerful force in its own right, and even without purity, it can be made to serve evil purposes.

When desire is pure, an affinity, or a similarity, is established with the Light of Wisdom, and the similarity completes the connection. The closer we are to the Light, the closer we are to the Desire to Share, and hence, to intelligence. Closeness, in this case, has no reference to distance. When people are close to one another, it is because they share similar intelligences and Desires to Receive. So great is the power at this level that pure energies come into play, energies that are not in contest with things at the corporeal level. But how does one achieve such an altered state of consciousness? Rav Shimon bar Yochai had the answer. "Look around," he said, "because that is where you are going to find your answer."

Look around and find, for example, a walnut. It has a shell. Remove that shell and you have the internal aspect of the walnut. All physical forms have shells—even people. How often have you heard someone say in exasperation, "You simply cannot reach that person"? What does that mean? On a physical level, certainly the person in question can be reached. He can be touched, pushed, smitten, or caressed, but move one step up the ladder to the metaphysical level and you will detect the magnetic field he has built around himself to keep others out. This is his shell.

Shells can be very thick indeed. They prevent us from getting deep into the interior of whatever they surround, and at both the physical and metaphysical level, such shells are constructed of the Desire to Receive, which is the exact opposite of inner consciousness, which is the Desire to Share. The two desires are not on similar frequencies. They are on frequencies far apart, and as a result, there is less revealment of the energy involved. The only way that an ESP connection can be made is for us to connect with our self, eliminating much of our own Desire to Receive and thus grow spiritually. Spiritual growth means nothing more than getting closer to the ultimate Vessel, which reveals the Light. When we speak of a person who manages to achieve greater alternate states of consciousness, we really are discussing someone capable of connecting to the frequency, or channel, of an increasingly pure vessel, and the purer the vessel, the greater the amount of the Light of Wisdom it will reveal. The degree to which one can tap into this energy will depend upon the degree to which physicality is diminished.

It is not easy to achieve this diminution. It requires a conscious effort on the part of the person who first must rid himself of his inborn Desire to Receive for the Self Alone. This is accomplished through prayer and meditation, which may be launched by the beginner as a program of halting all extraneous thought for ten minutes a day as he seeks the multitude of levels of frequencies by which his desire may be accomplished. To halt thought, however—to turn off the constant internal dialogue that all of us carry on constantly with ourselves—is the equivalent of halting a runaway team of horses. It can be done, but only with deep dedication and long practice. This is not the place to delve into kabbalistic meditation, a subject fit for another volume. Suffice it to say that we must conquer physicality before we can achieve the altered state of consciousness necessary to move beyond it.

The difference between a computer mainframe and its microchips is physicality. The less the physicality—and as microchips dwindle toward the molecular level, computers become increasingly powerful—the greater the similarity to the internal energy that does not move and has no speed of its own but exists rather as pure frequency. It may appear to the observer at the physical level that movement takes place, but the energy is there in total pervasiveness all the time, transcending the concept of light speed.

With these points established, we now can begin to understand the meaning of Creation in the Bible. We are told in *Genesis* 5:6, of people living at the time of Adam and for several generations thereafter who enjoyed extraordinarily long lifetimes. Adam lived 930 years, and Methuselah held the record at 976. Mankind's life expectancy subsequently declined to an average span of 40 years (although in the past century, this has gradually begun to rise again), but the Bible addresses neither phenomenon because the Bible is generally not concerned with recorded history. Genesis, rather, reveals coded phenomena designed to explain parallel universes, metaphysics, and other frames of reference, including the Age of Aquarius in which we now live and in which technological advances of the past 30 years far exceed any that took place in the millennia of the past.

Many things called unknown or unknowable by modern man are revealed in the Bible, but we shall deal here only with a few of these through our explanation of the all-pervading energy of intelligence that offers itself to all of us for beneficial connection. One problem, for example, that has baffled mankind in general and scientists in particular for years is the sudden extinction of the dinosaurs after what scientists tell us was 150 million years of rule. The list of suspected reasons for their demise is as long as human ingenuity can make it, but all the theories have one thing in common, and that is catastrophe.

While the harebrained ideas of such mavericks as Immanuel Velikovsky in his book *Worlds in Collision* have shown the importance of catastrophe as a means of evolutionary change, none have really achieved scientific acceptance. This is because the aim of science is to discover only those natural laws that function with precise of order. If such were the sole stock of the Creator, the principles of evolution would be rigid with regularity. In the scientific view, some unsettling, freakish extraterrestrial event that put an end to millions and millions of years of orderly evolution just doesn't seem to be the proper answer. And in this case, the scientists are right.

The truth is that the dinosaurs never were and are not now extinct. We have lived among them for centuries, simultaneously blessing them for their favors and regarding them with primordial fear. We call them reptiles.

The Bible tells us that before the fall of Adam, "there were giants on the Earth in those days," (*Numbers* 13:33) and indeed there were. The coding in Genesis tells us that Adam himself may have towered 100 feet tall[5] in the metaphysical paradise of Eden where he and Eve reigned in complete obedience to the laws of nature and the universe until the Desire to Receive for Oneself Alone overcame them. With the Fall, however, their world dwindled, diminishing both in stature and in the Light of Wisdom, until Adam was but a weary farmer of our accustomed physical proportion, tilling the soil in a field where the once-great dinosaurs now skittered and slithered as innocuous lizards and snakes. You may not find *Tyrannosaurus Rex* in the meadow, but you will find the pathetic remnant of his progeny, not extinct but utterly unrecognizable. If this flies in the face of Darwin's explanation of evolution, so be it, but it also explains for the fundamentalists why no thunder lizards trod the gangplank of Noah's Ark.

The foregoing may strike the average person, locked as he is in his linear world of time, space, and motion, as the image of a febrile mind, but in the kabbalistic world view, there are many different universes, different veils, and different cosmic influences that structure different kinds of life, both on the metaphysical and physical planes. We find in the *Zohar*[6] and in the *Gates of Reincarnation* by Rav Isaac Luria, that every man contains multiple levels of parallel universes and only in this context can the code of Genesis be understood. The lower level of man's multiplicity is called Crude Spirit (*Nefesh*). Above that lies another sphere called Spirit (*Ruach*) and the upper level is called Soul (*Neshamah*). Within this context, Kabbalah introduces a new way of thinking about old concepts. For example, within the levels of parallel universes lies parallel states of consciousness that lead mankind back to various levels of the Desire to Receive, which, in itself, is a consciousness, which is further divided into infinite levels.

This path leads us to the answer to the paradox discussed earlier concerning time travel and the speed of light. When we approach the speed of light in the Einsteinian sense, space and time cease to exist. At this point, time travel, at the level of consciousness where time ceases to be, can begin. This is the phase at which the level of gravitation, which effectively prohibits acceleration of space and time, also vanishes in a gravitational field. In the parallel universes of the metaphysical, time travel begins above Crude Spirit; Pure Spirit reigns. Upon reaching the level of Spirit, the individual enters into a new level or an altered state of consciousness that consists of pure awareness, which alters the level of his

Desire to Receive, bringing it into harmony with the Light of Wisdom, which has only one characteristic: Desire to Share, which is not governed by space-time and which can exist only at the level of limitation. Within the Light of Wisdom, nothing is lacking, and when we reach this level, finally bereft of the Desire to Receive for Ourselves Alone, we have made the outer-space connection.

Once this connection is made—through prayer, meditation, and a conscious determination to restrict the Desire to Receive (which is, by the way, our sole possible exercise of free will)—past events can literally be witnessed either as flashes from previous incarnations or through dreams that can illuminate the future as well as the past. Such revelations lie in the spiritual realm of Spirit (*Ruach*), in which there is no manifestation of time, space, or motion as we perceive them in *Nefesh*, the Crude Spirit realm where most of us dwell. *Nefesh* alone allows the body to age and deteriorate. In *Nefesh* alone can there be lies, deceit, and death, along with that sense of mortality that limits human vision to the here and now. The soul that can rise to the parallel universe of *Ruach*, where Adam lived before the Fall, is affected by nothing in *Nefesh*, which explains why the so-called grandfather paradox is no paradox at all. Any adventurer going back in time to prevent the marriage of his grandparents would have to do so in the realm of *Ruach*, and the physical union of his grandparents never existed there in the first place.

The key to time travel at the level of *Ruach* is the ability to share; nothing else will put the soul in close proximity to the

Light of Wisdom. Once enveloped in that all-pervasive, motionless light, perceptions of time and space fade like dreams, and all the time traveler must do to witness the signing of the Magna Carta or see Moses receiving the Ten Utterances is to decide that he is at Runnymede or on Mount Sinai. Given such travel arrangements, I may say that I saw you at a given time on a certain street corner and you may protest that you were not there. Further inquiry, however, may reveal that you thought, even for a fleeting moment, of the location or planned to go there in the future, so that would be the moment I saw you. Time travel is literally at the fingertips of anyone who is willing to let him- or herself be free of the Desire to Receive for Oneself Alone and thereby find the true Desire to Share all that he can obtain from the Light of Wisdom.

Before the sin of Adam (which was a "negation of the Light of Wisdom), the entire world existed at the level of *Ruach*, unfettered by the chains of space and time and unshadowed by entropy and death. When Adam fell spiritually, he literally fell from the blessed state of consciousness of *Ruach* into *Nefesh*, dragging the world down with him. We, his descendants, have been struggling ever since to regain the Eden of the Creation. We have failed simply because we have never realized one central truth, that most of the tragedies that befall us do so because we have blindly and carelessly willed them to by the power of our words. God created the cosmos with a word, and that power, diluted many times by our own egocentric Desire to Receive with little thought of imparting, was passed on to us, His creatures.

We learn from the *Zohar* that we must be very careful with how we address catastrophe, illness, or other life-threatening situations. To speculate verbally as to what might happen activates another state of consciousness that almost inevitably creates the occurrence being so fearfully discussed. The thought becomes the reality; the word becomes the deed. There are many such states of consciousness, and not all of them are benign. But because man never can separate himself from the universe, all of these states, even the lowest, contain power that only fools will trifle with. The soul's only defense as it journeys through the myriad levels that make up the metaphysical universe is to achieve at-one-ment (remove the hyphens and receive yet another word of power—atonement) with the Light of Wisdom.

One of the best road maps clarifying the way to this goal is kabbalistic astrology as explained by this passage in the *Zohar*:

> As the body of man is divided and subdivided into sections and all are poised upon levels of different magnetic fields and intelligence, by which each react and interact with the other, although remaining independent, so is the entire world based upon parallel and different levels by which each section, each segment of the universe is related and interrelated with each other. And upon man rests the entire movement and strings of the universe.[7]

50

Here are two incredible statements: Man is the determining director of movement in the universe, and man is structured as a carbon copy of everything in that universe! Science probes for the answers that religion takes on faith, and astrology is the bridge between them.

To date, for all our technological advances, the only place where man has walked beyond the Earth is its moon. Astrology permits one to go further; to acquire knowledge about all the other planets in the solar system and to determine the extent of their astral influences. The pure scientist may shake his head in despair at such a statement, but once again, the *Zohar* makes it clear: "The body of man is related to our entire galaxy and universe." In-depth analysis of the body, along with understanding which planet or which part of our galaxy relates to each different section of man, the different parts of man will open new vistas to the Heavens. We can then, with proper analysis and investigation from a kabbalistic point of view, probe and penetrate the inner depths, those internal energy forces of the different parts of the body. And thus, in this way, the kabbalist is in a position to understand the internal energy force and intelligence of the planets.

In this age of quantum mechanics and microchips, the education of an individual cannot possibly be complete without some knowledge of the basic fundamentals of science and its historical background. What the *Zohar* presents opens to both the layman and the scientist of tomorrow a new understanding of the laws of nature and of the theory of relativity. The theory of relativity touches many aspects of the physical world, ranging from the atomic realm to the make-up of the universe. The *Zohar* repeatedly states: "That which is below is above, and that which is above is below."[8] Reinforced by the theory of relativity, everything really is connected and interdependently related. The revelation of the *Zohar* allows us, through careful scrutiny of the anatomy of the individual, to learn exactly what exists both in the realm of the known galaxy and in the realm of undiscovered celestial objects as well.

It, therefore, comes as no surprise that the famed Italian Kabbalist Shabbatai Donolo was also a physician. Donnolo studied medicine, pharmacology, astronomy, and astrology. He was well-versed in the *Talmud* and knew Hebrew, Aramaic, Italian, Greek, and Latin. Donnolo set out his idea of a divinely created universe, with man in the image of God. His famous work on Kabbalah, referred to as the Book of Wisdom, explains in precise detail the composition and relationship of one planet to another. Donolo's *Book of Remedies*, contains a great deal of material drawn from his knowledge of astrology, a knowledge undoubtedly based upon his comprehension of Kabbalah.

Donolo's *Book of Wisdom* provides a mass of information on the study of astrology. Without this thorough insight into the essential and fundamental structures and composites of our great galaxy, astrology would remain incomprehensible, and the study of the Heavens would remain dichotomous, with astrology and science separated as to what constitutes the universe. Donolo's information paves the way for the study of astrology to finally become a respected science.

The origins of astrology, and hence of astronomy, are lost in the mists of time. When man first attempted to arrange the structure of his life, his attention naturally was drawn to the Heavens, which seemed to hold the key to structural order. The regular cycle of day and night and the steady rhythm of the seasons were reason enough to look skyward. What was lost, even though it has existed since the time of Abraham's *Book of Formation*, were the formulae that explained it all.

As a result of that loss, worship of the stars came into being. One who delved into the science and study of astrology was considered an idol worshipper, which from a kabbalistic viewpoint is far from the truth. When man accepted the sun, stars, and planets as deities to be worshipped for the benefits they might bestow, they worshipped these bodies for a specific reason: They wanted to make use of celestial bodies for personal gain. The physical beneficence alone of the celestial bodies was considered. No one really attempted to make an in-depth study of the internal, or spiritual, structure, and through that narrow view of the Heavens, the truth was lost.

Early civilizations considered the celestial deities to be their rulers. They accepted the proposition that astral influences existed, but that they could do little to overcome them. Thus misinformation began to creep in. From a kabbalistic point of view, if astral influences were negative, how to jam or deflect them became of paramount importance, and prayer swiftly became the vehicle by which the supplicant hoped to achieve that power. The Hebrew word for prayer is *tafel*, which literally means "secondary, a reflection, the periphery." Prayer is not central to the issue. Prayers are merely channels, and like a driverless vehicle or a telephone line with no speaker to use it, prayers become a nullity. The business of prayer still remains big business in the modern world of religion, but like its idolatrous root, which turned such stars as Betelgeuse or Altair into gods and put a deity named Apollo into the cockpit of the sun, prayer is a myth.

Prayer, from a kabbalistic point of view, is merely a tapping of energy, just as the aforementioned stars are bottled-up energies in a metaphysical cosmos. Prayer is not an appeal to a higher court; a plea for mercy, justice, or gain. The kabbalist knows the channels that convey the only power worth having, the one that neutralizes the Desire to Receive for the Self Alone. This is the crippler that renders what the religious call "prayer" to little more than empty rhetoric. Pity the man who anchors the destiny of his soul in the shifting, treacherous sands of what men call prayer.

Prayer is a powerful thing, but unhappily, few know how to wield it. Even as we engage in prayer, our minds wander far afield, planning schedules for the next day, worrying about business or simply daydreaming. As a body of people, Jews prayed fervently during the Holocaust, but that did not save six million from the crematoria. Many prayed while a similar holocaust annihilated the nation of Cambodia, but prayer apparently rescued few of Pol Pot's victims. This is because prayer is all a question of technology and connecting to proper channels. If I want to watch the 11 o'clock news and I tune in at 9 o'clock, I will not receive the program sought, no matter how fervently I desire it. If I insist on watching Channel 2, all the power of technology will not permit me to see programming on Channel 4. Every two hours, our prayers are influenced by a different planet. To pray effectively, we must know, be connected to, and understand the correct planetary influence. Otherwise, our efforts are worth little more than idol (or idle) worship.

To overcome the old false gods who, like the human souls who invented them, seem to reincarnate through the ages in one form or another, one must use any number of the keys offered by Kabbalah. One of the most effective keys on the ring is astrology, once its internal spiritual structure is revealed. Astrology is both a science and an art, but the mechanics of its science as well as the techniques of its art are bound to the understanding and interpretation of the internal cosmic influence that the heavenly bodies have on the individual. We must, therefore, know about the scientific basis of astronomy to understand why the universe is structured as it is. We must achieve a thorough understanding of *why* celestial bodies behave the way they behave as well as the relationship between the way they behave and the position they find themselves in at any given time. Then, and only then, can we hope to bridge the astrology/astronomy gap and consider them as one science, not two. This is important because observable behavioral patterns are merely manifestations of their celestial bodies. What is crucial is to seek new answers to Kabbalah's most important question: Why?

The answer lies in the metaphysical concept that the seed becomes the tree, thus demonstrating that that which is revealed must first be concealed. The primary cause, however, still remains after manifestation, as does the seed, once planted, forever concealed. How often have you done or said something totally unplanned and unexpected and then wondered, often ruefully, why you did it? You may examine your mind without finding the seed of the action. The "seed" did its work, but it remains hidden. Yet the key to understanding is no longer hidden. Kabbalistic astrology, backed by the *Sefer Yetzirah*, the earliest known work of Judaic mysticism, can serve as the road map to motives. The *Sefer Yetzirah* is remarkable in that it provides most of the answers that are necessary to establish astrology as a science.

The enormous growth and popularity astrology has enjoyed in the last 20 years is probably related to the Age of Aquarius. The fact that astrology became acceptable, even respectable in the latter half of the 20th century can be traced to Aquarian influence. Nor is it by chance that the knowledge of Kabbalah became widespread and available to the layman at the same time. Ancient secrets are now available to all, and it is no longer necessary to accrue vast amounts of knowledge before delving into them.

Through the scientific structure provided by the *Sefer Yetzirah* and the many commentaries written on it, it is my hope that a proper understanding of the system may be rendered, and while I do not deny that one can achieve much knowledge and help through the conventional path of astrology, I must stress the dichotomy between science and astrology. This gap cannot be completely bridged unless and until there is an in-depth understanding of astronomy and the universe with all its physical bodies. Kabbalah takes this one giant step forward, allowing a greater number of "whys" still facing and perplexing the scientific community to be answered.

Far-reaching changes in recent years seem to hold great promise for the progress of astrology. They inevitably will change attitudes toward its serious study. The use of natural explanations serves to relate astrology to the scientific community, and this book will identify a great deal of the common ground between the two. According to the *Zohar*, the rhythms and cycles of the universe have a profound impact upon the rhythms and cycles of biology and anatomy. A sincere and successful partnership between astrology and science is likely to result through the dissemination of this information.

Unhappily, at the moment, astrology and Kabbalah share one unfortunate attribute in the public mind: Neither is believed. Kabbalah is as much scorned on principle by many who have never heard the word as it is by those who have heard only the word. Reactions range from fear to humanistic pragmatism, but lack of belief predominates, all of which is sheer folly because to use the word "believe" is to admit that one does not know. Thus, despite the recent popularization of astrology, attitudes toward it in many quarters are based not upon what it is known, but upon what is not known. The *Zohar* passage I am about to quote will rankle many astrologers and true believers, even though I do not necessarily find any contradiction here between the *Zohar* and conventional astrology: "And the wisdom of their wisdom was lost…" The *Zohar* states[9] that "was lost" refers to the wisdom of the ancient Egyptians whose innate understanding has forever been concealed, even though the Egyptians in the day of their power did not realize it. The *Zohar* goes on to explain: "… for they do not know in the initial creation of celestial bodies, but only in their manifested uses. Their knowledge is based on the changes that are observed in the world we experience, in their travel, and in the way they are made use of."

Thus, from the *Zohar*, we arrive at the correct conclusion that the ancient Egyptians' philosophy of astrology was not based on the internal structure of creation, meaning the original "Why?" Knowledge is the mother of creation as well as invention, and this is where the action really exists. This, no less than the seed or the sperm, is the cause of the ultimate effect.

The *Zohar* here merely follows the general pattern of duality upon which all creation is constructed: the physical and the metaphysical, the external and the internal. Man, in whom we perceive both a body and a soul, is no differently structured than creation as a whole. The objective, therefore, of kabbalistic astrology as it is approached in this book is to reveal both the internal and external composites of the entire universe, including man.

Once we have acquired this knowledge, we will be on the threshold of a major breakthrough in interplanetary communication. According to Kabbalah, all transfers of energy are, in effect, transfers of intelligence. To speak of extraterrestrial "intelligent life" is to speak of nothing more than just this fact. No little green men or spaceships roaring in warp drive out of *Star Trek* are necessary. Transfers of energy, transfers of information, however, are made throughout the universe, and where there is a transfer of information, intelligence becomes a power. "Mind power" can therefore no longer be excluded from the realm of scientific inquiry.

Kabbalah has given us the names whereby we can pinpoint any particular exchange of energy, rendering interplanetary communication, with its transfer of energy/information, no more wondrous than a similar transfer made between individuals over a telephone. Much has been made in the past 20 years of signals that seem to be coming from interstellar space. Most of these signals have been traced to such enigmatic phenomena as quasars or pulsars, with little credence given to the possibility of other civilizations as a source. From a kabbalistic point of view, no such civilizations exist beyond the confines of the planet Earth, but that does not mean that the signals first detected by such endeavors as Project Ozma are devoid of true, and useful, intelligence. Intelligence is simply the kind of energy that is manifested at one point and perceived at another point at a given time. There is nothing random or unchoreographed about the dance of the electrons that comprise the cosmos.

The kabbalist knows how to tap into the forces of intelligence that pervade the universe. All of these forces have names, set forth as the *Sefirot* in the Tree of Life. The *Sefirot* are channels that carry such concepts as judgment, mercy, wisdom, and victory, much the same way a cable carries electrical current. Make no mistake, however, they are very real. Every event, every action, every idea is connected through the human mind by the network that is the cosmos. Space is mind, and we are part of it, but Western science has no idea what or where the mind is.

Let us examine the full range of this power. Humans always have controlled it, but in nearly all cases, without conscious intent. We remember with horror the Holocaust of World War II, but do we remember the festering hatred that caused it? Every action of man is carried by the channels of the cosmos whether man knows it or not. Every earthquake, every supernova, every war is the direct result of violence and hatred in the hearts of men. We have at our fingertips the ability to recreate Eden. Instead, we build nuclear warheads and prepare for unspeakable hell.

Every one of us participates in this process. Negative thinking triggers negative action, just as positive thinking triggers positive action. Unhappily, we seem to prefer the negative, and in a world as small as ours, the impact of such negativity is massive. The slightest deception, the pettiest crime, the smallest injustice committed by the least of us is part and parcel of a world conspiracy of hatred that can and will, if not turned around, eventually destroy the world. Control of the negative was the means by which Egypt enslaved the world prior to the *Exodus*. Can any of us take lightly the thought that any autocratic country would do no less today, given such power and the conscious control of it?

Here, then, is what kabbalists have known for centuries, and what scientists well might discover: One star appears on the Sabbath, and it is this star that deactivates the Desire to Receive on the metaphysical plane where, the *Zohar*[10] tells us, there are 70 stars, representing seven *Sefirot* and offering 70 facets of evil and 70 of good. They do cosmic battle every Friday, and if the unconscious actions of man sway that battle what might the conscious actions of those who select evil as the means to their ends accomplish? Answer this question and suddenly the mere physicality of a nuclear detonation becomes little more than a footnote in this tale of terror.

The concept of the reality of anything physical has changed considerably since the discovery of modern quantum theory. Originally, the physical universe and our thoughts about it were believed unrelated and separate. Quantum physics shows us that what we can visualize actually is what we can see. Our mental picture of the universe and the way the universe appears to us are essentially one and the same. The world of thought is not isolated from the physical world, but is, on the contrary, closely bound up in it. Through our five senses, the mind is the recipient of a constant flow of information and of intelligent life forms of energy. The mind stimulates the manifestation of either new thoughts or existing ones.

What, however, is the mind? This intriguing question has long been a favorite topic of debate among philosophers and religionists, and today, science studies the question through psychoanalysis and brain research. Though much seems to be obvious, the mechanism whereby matter acts upon the mind and, more importantly, that triggers the mind and its mental activity into the physical expression of mind over matter remains one of the most elusive phenomena facing the scientific community. How far does mind power extend? What are its limitations? Where, precisely, is the power of the mind located?

Wherever the answers lie, one thing is certain: Intelligence, or mind power, does exist. The French geneticist François Jacob once said that "the reason physics became ruler of the pack was that physics was the first to have its own language," referring to the language of mathematics. But then something happened. We discovered a world beyond our five senses and everything changed. The language of mathematics was no longer capable of addressing thought, metaphysics, or the unseen but still very real world. The principle of uncertainty prevails, and there no longer is a language to explain it away. It becomes dizzying to think of mass and particles that exist, yet patently do not exist, and this forces any good theoretical physicist to let go of solid ground and learn to become a mystic. In this, the kabbalistic view becomes the only logic. The entire intelligence system of the universe, with its multiplicity of signals, is the direct result of the actions of man and therefore provides a complex interface of man's behavior.

Star Wars, whether the property of George Lucas or Ronald Reagan, is nothing new. Star Wars, in their broadest sense,

was even common in Moses' day, as this passage from the
Zohar[11] indicates:

> And Moses assembled the children of Israel separately
> and gave them the Sabbath anew, saying, "Six days
> shall work be done. Do not kindle any fire throughout
> your domain upon the Sabbath day." Herein lies the
> supreme mystery, revealed only to those versed in the
> Supreme Wisdom. On the sixth day, when nightfall is
> due to begin, a brilliant star appears in the north
> accompanied by seventy other stars. That star smites the
> others, absorbing them all into itself, so that one takes
> the place of all seventy. The same star becomes enlarged
> and becomes a fiery mass, blazing on all sides. The
> flaming mass then extends itself around a thousand
> mountains which ultimately becomes a mere thread.
> After this, the fiery mass draws out from within itself a
> variety of colors. The first is a green color and when the
> green color appears, the fiery mass raises itself and
> plunges into the midst of the green color, establishing its
> presence within the case of it. Then the fiery mass of the
> star attracts within its interior a white cosmic color
> force. It then ascends and again invades the inner
> cosmic energy force of that color, occupying its internal
> cosmic center. The same cosmic event occurs with all
> known colors, all of which it thrusts outside, focusing
> itself more intensely toward the middle until it
> approaches that hidden point where the energy center
> exists and derives its light there from.

This amazing and profound section of the *Zohar* not only provides a new dimension of the subatomic world, but it focuses upon the enormous influence and power of astral-body intelligence as well. The real Star Wars is the battle of man that becomes manifest on a planetary level. The signals we seem to be receiving from other civilizations are really transfers of energy that originated right here on Earth and have become manifest at all levels. The higher the level, the lesser the material aspect and the more refined the energy itself is. Thus, as noted in the *Zohar*, Earth-time and man's behavior produce an incredible energy reaction and interaction at the cosmic level. And at that level, the refinement of the cosmic consciousness of purer vessels inevitably produces greater intensities of energy transfer and revealment.

It is important to remember that cosmic events illustrated by the parable of the *Zohar* always have been and always will be under human control, albeit most of the time without conscious intent. The Nazi Holocaust was not merely a random horror. It was the result of a building hatred that became a channel for mass murder. We have at our fingertips the means by which we could recreate an Eden on Earth simply by benevolent mass action, but that will not happen until mankind understands that through the mass action of hatred and violence, we are creating just the opposite. Nations go on building nuclear warheads—and with them, a cataclysm that could end the human race—but in a world as small as ours, even the tiniest crime or negative thought helps fuel the race toward death, even as the level of pure awareness eludes us.

It does not elude the kabbalist, however, nor does it have to necessarily remain beyond the reach of any of us. In an altered state of consciousness, time ceases to be a factor, and the perceived lag between cause and effect vanishes with it. The Age of Aquarius influence finds our civilization preoccupied with rational science. Our entire civilization will be dominated by and based upon science and technology, but those disciplines ultimately must rest upon the humanity of Aquarius, which is depicted by the symbol of this sign of the zodiac. Aquarius is a human figure shown in a kneeling position, urn of cosmic water rests upon one shoulder with contents flowing out in front of him.

The internal consciousness of this 11th sign of the zodiac is simple. According to the *Zohar*[12] and the *Book of Formation*, the inner recesses of cosmic Aquarian thought hold the elements of sharing, Right Column, and humanity. Sharing consciousness is an understanding of the oneness of all mankind which in turn, indicates that Aquarius represents the dissemination of knowledge and the sharing of thought energy telepathically through brain waves.[13] Thus, Aquarius has become associated with the Space Age when communication through the media contains less of the physical corporeal material of that function than in times past. The Aquarian is involved with people. "Love thy neighbor" (*Leviticus* 19:18) is his motto, and there are no boundaries to be considered. Space is the limit for the power of water, which is the sharing concept. The Aquarian Age, therefore, is the true harbinger of knowledge, for in this 11th sign, the Desire to Receive continues to diminish. It is precisely for this reason that this sign is closely associated with the coming of the Age of the

Messiah—the stripping away of the limitations of man, thereby paving the road to universal freedom.

Our present-day high-tech society, therefore, has emerged as a direct result of the Aquarian Age. Cosmically, it is the symbol of high-speed communication via space-borne satellite and of the removal of the dense corporeality that marked earlier heavy and cluttered systems. For the first time in history, we are experiencing a diminution of that internal intelligence that is Desire to Receive for Oneself Alone, and the result is seen not only in permutations of rational science, but in an unprecedented interest in spiritual teachings and in the love movements of recent decades. From the flower power of the 1960s to the microchip of the 1980s, all may be attributed directly to the astral influence of the Age of Aquarius.

Science is not the cause of these changes, nor will science be the cause of ultimate human relationships that hopefully will result in a grand tearing down of barriers between man and his fellow man—barriers constructed of the desire Desire to Receive for Oneself Alone—between man and his fellow man. People, however, will always be the determining factor as to where this manifestation of the Aquarian Age will lead us. Will science and technology be harnessed for peaceful purposes, leading us to interdependency, interrelationships, and inseparableness, or will they fail the golden potential of the age because mankind fails the challenge of the age?

From a kabbalistic point of view, all things now lead in one direction: Quantum, the objective of which is "love thy neighbor." When this goal is achieved by mankind, the entire universe—both the seen and the unseen—will be revealed as they presently exist as a single, unified whole. Our universe is perceived as fragmented only because mankind is fragmented.

All technology, all of science and its direction, including the movement of the stars (and the war of stars), will be completely dependent upon the actions of man and his relationship and interrelationship with that which is around him. If the relationship of humankind becomes manifested within a concept of "love thy neighbor," then we can be assured that the result will be one of science and technology meeting the needs and demands of our universe and providing peaceful, harmonious objectives rather than operating for the sake of science alone. If, on the other hand, we cannot learn to adjust, compromise, and live with our fellow man, then we will be the determining factor for science and technology to lead us into chaos and ultimate total destruction, which, as described in the *Zohar*[14], will be a horrible war of stars, which all of us will witness and which will be a result of and the culmination of our actions.

It is difficult for some scientists to accept the proposition that man is more than just another tiny speck in this infinite universe, with many universes (possibly containing far greater intelligence than our own) consisting of an admixture of physicality and the energy of the supernal and that one "remote control" called humanity is capable of influencing and directing all of them. Hopefully, with this knowledge, we can achieve the objective of "love thy neighbor" by making people more aware of what the real world is all about. By dedicating ourselves to the dissemination of a more all-embracing harmony in human affairs at the human level, we may learn to care for and understand each other.

"I DO NOT BELIEVE THAT GOD PLAYS DICE WITH THE UNIVERSE."

—Albert Einstein

CHAPTER THREE

ASTRAL INFLUENCES: GAMBLE OR GUARANTEE?

The importance of astral influences, stressed both by the Bible and the Zohar, makes it clear that "chance" is no answer to the question of why things happen to us. There are some bizarre coincidences that only astrology can explain. To illustrate the point, let us turn to the Bible and the phrase, "The children of Israel shall pitch by their own standard, with the flag according to their fathe"s house." (*Numbers* 2:1-2) Since there is no Hebrew word for "pitch," the word obviously stems from a corruption of translation. The proper translation is, "The children of Israel shall rest ..." What, then, is the significance of a flag? What is the origin of the tradition behind the flag or banner? From a kabbalistic point of view, the flag means more than just honor and ego, but if the Bible is a spiritual instrument, would the meaning of a flag not also display some form of spirituality?

The word, which is omitted in all translations of the Bible, is the same Hebrew word that appears in Genesis whenever the Bible discusses signs of the seasons, which is to say, signs of the zodiac. What then, is the relationship, if any, between the concept of the flag, signs of the zodiac and the statement "according to their father's house?" After asking these questions the *Zohar*[15] informs us that herein lies the secret of astrology—the internal creation of the signs.

Conventional astrology recognizes only the superficial external energy force field of astral signs and influences. The internal energy center and magnetic fields of the zodiac are completely forgotten. As the *Zohar* indicates, "The wisdom of their wise people will disappear. The intelligence of their intelligent people will be hidden." (*Isaiah* 29:14) Conventional astrology, therefore, brings a great number of contradictions, despite providing a great deal of service and insight because somewhere along the line, something has been lost.

This particular chapter of the *Zohar* indicates that the position of flags and encampments described in the Bible are directly related to the internal magnetic cosmic fields generated by signs of each constellation. It is in these verses that the true astral influences which relate to the positions of the tribes of Israel now are revealed in our generation fully and for the first time. Signs of the zodiac, symbolized by the tribes, were placed in a position establishing three in each of four directions forming the sides of a rectangle. They represent the four elements of the universe, with the air sign aligned to the east, the water sign to the south, the fire sign to the north and the earth sign to the west.

Thus, a seemingly insignificant passage in the Bible takes on a new depth of meaning which, hopefully, will permit conventional astrology to achieve its proper place among the sciences. Alignment of the tribes, representing elemental signs of the zodiac, symbolizes Israel's structure as a Three-Column System with positive and negative poles cosmically balanced by a central pillar. This is the weapon with which Moses took the Israelites out of bondage in Egypt and the power that still accrues to those who pursue and achieve mastery of its secrets, not the least of which is information relative to peoples who live, even now, in the east, west, north and south. By such means the validity of astrology is established.

Astrology combines the worlds of metaphysics and astral influences, the internal aspect of astrology with the science of astronomy, and the physical expression and manifestation of the internal with magnetic energy fields.

The infinite, vast and boundless, darkness is densely packed with infinite points of brightness which ultimately extend into billions of tiny glowing illuminations. These illuminations are themselves composed of an infinite number of radiant points of light which we know as stars. Why are stars there? Again the *Zohar*[16] explains, and in doing so, continues the validation of the influence of astral bodies:

> *Hence Solomon who knew everything, spoke thus:*
> *Now observe that all of the doings of the world are*
> *controlled by vast numbers of astral entities. But the*
> *people of the world know not and regard not what is*

that which upholds them. (Ecclesiastes 1:8) *Even Solomon, wisest of men, could not comprehend them.*

There is no grass below that does not have an astral spirit or force from above. This blade of grass cannot begin to reap life provided the astral force, a specific star, does not beat it and exclaim, "Now grow!"

Could there be a clearer indication of the importance of astral entities? Much greater are the forces of the planets and signs of the zodiac, which are so close to our universe that we cannot help but be influenced by the astral energy fields. Religion seems to be in opposition to the effects of astral influences and the study of astrology. Both religious, orthodox-oriented Jews and fundamentalist Christians seem to be extremely imbued with this sort of antagonistic attitude toward astrology—a mindset generally matched by educated atheists (and if atheism is not a religion, why do its practitioners preach it so fervently?). To these religionists, I would have to ask the same questions that the *Zohar* poses when it asks why the Jewish nation was born during the astral planetary influence of Mars. Why did the liberation of the Israelite—the emancipation from slavery—take place on the 15th day in the sign of the zodiac of Aries, the ram? Why are particular days chosen to commemorate and celebrate particular holidays? Is there any reason why the revelation on Mount Sinai occurred during the influence of Gemini? Is it by mere coincidence that the destruction of the Temple commenced during the month of the zodiac sign of Cancer and culminated with its total destruction during the month of Leo? Why is the first month of the year considered to be during the constellation of the month of Libra?

Ultimately, all people of all faiths will come to the realization that the Jewish religion is not just a collection of rituals and beliefs. It is, rather, an instrument for defining the universe and its various elements. Jewish holidays are merely a timetable for the comprehension of specific manifestations of cosmic energies.

The practice of following the signs of the zodiac is constantly mentioned in kabbalistic material. A vast body of writing exists concerning the constellations and the galaxy. Why would *Chanukah* and *Purim* necessarily take place under the influence of Jupiter, as stated in kabbalistic writings, or more particularly by Rav Isaac Luria? When we observe our constellations and their stars and see the structured order that exists in the skies, we can begin to appreciate the magnitude of our galaxy. Yet even now, opposition to such studies continues to deprive man of the opportunity, as stated by the *Zohar*[17], to know and understand his environment so that he no longer must be a victim of the whims of astral influence. Man is unique and can determine his own destiny, but he cannot expect to accomplish much without the mystical realities of astrology.

Those of us living today can credit ourselves with acquiring more knowledge and wisdom than all of our ancestors. We know there is an interplanetary relationship between the moon and the Earth, and yet for some strange reason, we remain oblivious to the extent of its mystery. For example, the time between 5:00 p.m. and 7:00 p.m. is a period when there is a greater fear of robbery and mugging. But why is this period so justifiably feared? Did criminals gather at some point at a convention to decide that the best time for crime lay between the hours of 5:00 p.m. and 7:00 p.m.? Why has no one suggested that the statistically provable rise in crime as sunset approaches is driven by a cosmic energy force that compels people so inclined to exercise the violence of their greed? The prime example is as old as the *Book of Exodus*, which tells us how the golden calf was built late in the afternoon during Moses' absence: "And when the people saw that Moses delayed to come down from the mount, the people gathered themselves together unto Aaron and said unto him, 'Make us a god who shall go before us.'" (*Exodus* 32:1)

The word "people," in this case, denotes the "mixed multitude," including all the sorcerers and magicians of Egypt who followed Moses on the Exodus[18]:

> *During the day, the wizards practiced their unholy arts from the beginning of the second half of the sixth hour to the commencement of the second half of the ninth hour, while the lesser magicians worked from the middle of the ninth hour until midnight. They did this because during these evening hours, certain negative astral influences were in ascendancy. The sorcerers tapped these sources of energy and used them to animate the golden calf.*

So as we can see, in this analysis of crime, the kabbalistic astrologer preceded the statistician by three and a half millennia.

Astrology is gradually being recognized as a vehicle of viable, scientific truth that encompasses knowledge of the entire electromagnetic field of our universe. There is growing awareness by scientists that man is truly a responsive element in the cosmos, but the forces that dictate man-inspired events remain largely unseen and unknown. For example, the inexorable pattern of Jupiter and Saturn coincides with the death in office of every American president elected in an election year ending in zero; indeed, some of these presidents even studied the pattern in an effort to break the cycle. The presidential doom factor, however, lies less in the final digit of the election year than in the planetary conjunction that occurred at the time of the president's rise to office.

It really all began when William Henry Harrison was elected in 1840. He died of pneumonia in 1841. Twenty years later, in 1860, Abraham Lincoln was elected. He was assassinated in 1865. James A. Garfield was elected in 1880, 20 years after Lincoln won his first term; Garfield was assassinated in 1901. Warren Harding was elected in 1920 and died in office in 1923. In 1940, Franklin D. Roosevelt won his third term and died in office in 1945 during his fourth term. Then came John F. Kennedy, elected in 1960, only to be assassinated in 1963. In each case, these zero-year victors rose to the Oval Office when Jupiter and Saturn were in conjunction, an astral event that occurs every 20 years. If skeptics still are inclined to snort "mere coincidence," they will be hard-pressed to apply that misunderstood term to the bizarre Lincoln–Kennedy coincidence that stemmed from an unbreakable bond of destiny spanning more than a century and irrevocably connecting the lives of the two martyred presidents. How can this incredible set of circumstances be written off by any intelligent human as random occurrence?

The successors, of both Lincoln and Kennedy, were Southerners named Johnson, and both Johnsons had served in the U.S. Senate. Andrew Johnson, Lincoln's successor, was born in 1808 and Lyndon Johnson, who took the mantle from Kennedy, was born in 1908. Lincoln's assassin was born in 1839 and Kennedy's in 1939. Both assassins were murdered before they could be brought to trial.

Both Lincoln and Kennedy lost children while in the White House. John Wilkes Booth, Lincoln's assassin, shot his victim in a theater and fled to a warehouse. Lee Harvey Oswald shot Kennedy from a warehouse and fled to a theater. The full names of both assassins contain 15 letters, while the names of the succeeding vice presidents each had 13 letters. Both Lincoln and Kennedy were in their early 30s when they married, each to a beautiful 24-year-old brunette, both of whom spoke French fluently. Lincoln had a secretary named Kennedy who advised him not to attend the theater where he was assassinated. Kennedy had a secretary named Lincoln who urged him not to go to Dallas where he died. Lincoln had a cousin who became a U.S. senator and another cousin who was mayor of Boston. Another relative,

Levi Lincoln, was a Harvard graduate who became U.S. attorney-general and Robert Lincoln, the president's son, was ambassador to London for four years.

John F. Kennedy's relatives held similar positions in government. Teddy Kennedy was a U.S. senator from Massachusetts. Robert Kennedy, also a Harvard graduate, became attorney-general, then a U.S. senator from New York. John Kennedy's grandfather was mayor of Boston and his father was ambassador to London. Both Lincoln and Kennedy competed for vice-presidential nominations a century apart, in 1856 and 1956, and the presidential campaigns of both were marked by dramatic debates: Lincoln with Stephen A. Douglas, and Kennedy with Richard M. Nixon. Both presidents were deeply involved with civil rights for Blacks, both were shot in the back of the head in the presence of their wives, and both died on Friday. Such an uncanny series of coincidences involving the lives and deaths of our 16th and 35th presidents cannot be shrugged off lightly or dismissed casually. The same negative cosmic influences have overshadowed the lives of presidents elected in zero years. Kennedy and Lincoln, with a reincarnate link between them, were effectively handed the same program cassette and with little choice beyond some minor restructuring, had to live it out. The powers that propel such things have not changed since they were manifested in Moses' day, which takes us back to the making of the golden calf in the *Book of Exodus*. It is with less spectacular results but with identical motive that today's criminals, ignorant of what they are doing, take the same evening route to evil.

Can things really happen by chance? There must be some underlying explanation for such bizarre coincidences involving events separated by time and space. Common sense alone would deny that ungoverned chance by itself could be responsible for such an interlocking series of events as those that marked the lives of Lincoln and Kennedy a century apart. Correlation, not random chance, alone can be responsible for such a thing.

Science considers this a connecting principle: If A causes B, then A must occur in time before B. Synchronous happenings (*syn* meaning "together" and *chronous* meaning "time") occur regularly from year to year, and such synchronicity lies at the very heart of the science of astrology. Things that happen through a conjunction of events, whether they take place in time only a moment apart or are centuries removed from each other, are intimately connected. Once a contract has been made, that contract continues to influence, whether it is a legal document, a manifestation of metaphysics, or a scientific axiom.

In the 1920s, Werner Heisenberg discovered that since we cannot measure both the position and the momentum of any object in this universe with exact precision, the very concepts of position and momentum were thrown into doubt. This was a radical change in basic physics that shook the foundation of the scientific community. Heisenberg's uncertainty principle focused attention as never before on the intimate relationship between the observer and the world as we see it. Known as quantum theory, it forms a basis in what subsequently became known as the age of new physics. It provided the most impressive scientific evidence yet that consciousness plays an essential, if not a deciding role in the nature of physical reality.

All of this originally began with attempts by the scientific community to mechanize the thought-processes of logic and reasoning. The ability to reason usually has been claimed to be the single element that distinguishes man from other species. Nevertheless, it had often been considered that reason is a patterned process governed to some extent by conditional laws. But when paradoxes popped up so easily in set theory, doubt began to taint all of mathematics. Before atomic uncertainty became reality, it was assumed that all material objects obeyed and complied with the laws of mechanics. It was discovered, however, that the atomic world appeared fuzzy and at times full of chaos. Particles at the atomic level no longer appeared to follow a well-defined trajectory, and subatomic particles refused to be pinned down.

Heisenberg's uncertainty principle is the basic ingredient of the whole of quantum mechanics, taking us directly to the consequences of unpredictability and thus of questionability. Suddenly, it could be seen that events may occur without a cause. Quantum seems to break the causal principle by allowing things to happen with no apparent reason. Scientists now have accepted atomic uncertainty as truly intrinsic to nature.

But Albert Einstein's opinion that "God does not play dice with the universe" has little to do with what constitutes reality. To suddenly fall back on so flimsy an argument—that within the Divine, we will find our answers—does not seem to fit the description of a scientist. The centrality of the issue is the daring question of whether the atom is "something" or whether it is just an abstract construct of our imagination. Maybe it is just a thought, but if so, whose thinking lies behind the effect? If this "something" really exists as a separate entity, then at the very minimum, it should have a definite position and momentum.

To further confuse the issue, the famous Danish physicist Neils Bohr in *Atoms Physics and the Description of Nature*, said, "If you don't see it, it isn't there." But surely the world out there exists whether or not we are looking at it. The chair I am sitting on may have disappeared subatomically, but I am not likely to fall on the floor because of this. By confusing the distinction between subject and object, or between cause and effect, we seem to strongly suggest that consciousness, or the mind element, is essential to our observation of the real world.

If this is true, however, then the question that must be raised is whether or not the observer and the intelligence necessary for the act of observation need be human. Will the artificial intelligence of the computer eventually suffice? This question leads us back to the discussion of what and where the mind may be. Does consciousness have any influence over the physics or chemistry of the corporeal body? The answer is as simple as the law of action and reaction. If the body acts on the mind, then it must follow that the mind acts on the body. Yet from a kabbalistic point of view, the soul or mind always has the potential ability to govern the internal force of the body, that unseen force that is the Desire to Receive for the Self Alone. Free will is alive and well, so, in effect, how can any concept really be given a name? This aspect of uncertainty really means that no matter how accurately one tries to measure the classical quantities of position and momentum, there always will be an uncertainty in the measurement. As Heisenberg observed, predicting the future of atomic particles is impossible under these circumstances.

There is no question that this sort of thinking about the cosmos is new to the Western mind. The physicist now discovers that the very act of observing the atomic world introduces a kind of duality; a paradoxical way of seeing things.

Thus, when we consider coincidence separated by time and space, both of which are relative—the coincidence in question can be true because of astrological positioning. Because of zodiacal positions and their influence at any time, any strange series of interrelated events such as those linking the lives and deaths of Lincoln and Kennedy can occur. As Heisenberg wrote, "The understanding is recognized even before it is understood in detail."

This concept can be thoroughly confusing for the layman, but it is necessary to refer to it to illustrate how little control we really exercise over our own destinies. More than 60 years ago, George Orwell created a signpost for our future with his ominous book 1984. By that awful date, he postulated humankind, as he had known it in 1943, would have ceased to exist—not in a universal holocaust, but in a manner far more subtle. Orwell was writing of the death of humanity without the firing of a single shot: A world populated by people who would go right on living, but since they had stopped thinking, they would be living in a world in which individual consciousness and free determination could no longer exist. In Orwell's vision of the future, the activities of all mankind would conform to and be directed by scientists through manipulation and a government policy encapsulated in the motto: "Big Brother Is Watching You."

Orwell was incredibly ingenious in formulating this silent holocaust, but he did not have to invent much of it. He had to look no further than the development of the new age of physics to see his terrible fairy tale and grim prophetic fantasies come to life. The individual seemed to gradually be losing control of himself and his environment. Science, which had previously seemed to be providing mankind with total solutions, was suddenly speaking in terms of uncertainty. And today, humankind goes right on fumbling unpredictably in a welter of indeterminism.

A few scientists today insist that changing such programmed behavior is vital to our survival, going so far as to recommend genetic engineering as an effective means to accomplish this. Increasing numbers of women turn to sperm banks, longing to be impregnated with the seed of a Nobel Prize winner in the hope that the child they bear may be intellectually gifted. If ever we do learn how to use genetic engineering to increase intelligence, grant longevity, or guarantee other traits providing an advantage in life, there will be no shortage of clients competing to take their place in line. On the dark side, however, those who reject the new technology may find their offspring condemned to subhuman status. Indeed, all this automated, robotized technology may give rise to a future featuring an underclass of humans so low in status as to seem inferior to the machine. Can it be that as machines evolve their own kind of artificial intelligence, people may become just another inferior form?

What seems to emerge from all this is man's inability to advance as quickly as the technology he himself is creating. We are told that our logical faculties arise only after the fact. Things happen long before they are rationally understood. If progress and development seem to point to humankind's inability to control its destiny, then free will vanishes and cosmic determinism may well become part of our inhabited universe. It will make little difference whether the determining entity is science, government, or the cosmos. The average human will have little, if any, say in the management of his daily affairs. It is almost as if technology may be just another extraterrestrial life form directing and dictating human destiny.

One point, however, should be made in favor of cosmic influence. Of the three determining entities mentioned, this one alone cannot be accused of harboring the dehumanizing and mechanistic aspects that science or government inevitably bring into the equation. While the cosmic effect is potentially more disastrous, it is nevertheless more subtle in nature.

Human beings are often seen today as little more than complex machines involuntarily caught up in a mammoth mechanistic universe. The future, we feel, is already out there like a great gear train just waiting for our personal cogs to mesh and turn toward already determined conclusions. If this is the case, however, are we really powerless to change it, or does the new physics, with its quantum uncertainty principle, pull the rug out from under our feet and make a strong case for free will that endows the individual with an important role in the nature of physical reality? What, then, is it going to be: Predeterminism or free will? How can we reconcile quantum uncertainty with predetermined astral or cosmic influences? If all things are predetermined, we have been placed upon a course of action that has been decided in advance of our existence. The concept of intelligence seems to exclude our participation in the cosmic plan, whereas the quantum principle undermines cosmic determinism inasmuch as the observer also is a participant.

Let us examine the position of determinism as it is understood by Kabbalah:

> Why should there be righteous men who are physical wrecks while many unrighteous men are hale and hearty?

> One explanation is that the latter were born of righteous parents while the former, though righteous themselves, were not children of righteous parents. The facts, however, militate against this since we see many righteous men who are the sons of righteous parents

who nevertheless are afflicted with bodily ills and are lifelong sufferers. There is a deep mystery here because all of God's pathways are based on truth and righteousness. In connection with this verse, I have found two mystical doctrines, each of which supports the other, in the books of the ancients. In essence, this is what they proclaim:

There is a period when the Moon is defective and judgment is visited upon her and the Sun is hidden from her. It is the moon that, in all times and seasons, releases souls to enter the sons of men, having previously gathered them for that purpose. A soul released during that period when the moon is under sentence—more specifically, when she begins to descend on the 15th day of the lunar month— everyone born at that particular time always will be the victim of degradation, poverty, and chastisement whether or not he is sinful or righteous. Those souls that the moon sends forth when she is in the grade of ascension and completeness and the perennially flowing stream plays upon her are destined to enjoy abundance of all good things—riches, children, and bodily health—all on account of the Mazal that flowed forth and joined itself to that grade in order to be perfected and blessed by it.

We thus see that all things are dependent upon Mazal astral influence by the dictum that "children, life, and livelihood" do not depend on man's merits, but on his astral influence, Mazal. Hence, all those who are sorely afflicted in this world, in spite of being truly righteous, suffer through the mischance of their souls.

What we learn from the foregoing *Zohar*[19] is that the constellations present constant forces in the universe, and planets present changing forces. The forces of the constellations can almost be pictured in physical terms as the carriers of the force, modulated by the play of planetary influences, all of which are exerted on the renewal and birth of souls.

Another indication of the link between astrology and science is provided in the *Zohar* when it discusses eclipses. In this case, the *Zohar* is concerned with an eclipse of the moon. If the eclipse occurs during the moon's ascent (the first 15 days of the month), the *Zohar*[20] says:

> *Because the moon is a composite of good and evil, it reflects the destinies of both Israel and Ishmael. When the moon is eclipsed in the time when ascending until she is full, it is an evil sign for Israel. However, when the moon is eclipsed at the time of its descent, it is an evil omen unto Ishmael.*

This clearly demonstrates the astral influence of the moon. We have a further demonstration of the link between astral influences and daily lifestyles in the same *Zohar*[21] section where it says:

"And God made two lights." The word *"made"* signifies the due expansion and establishment of the whole. The words *"two great lights"* show that at first they were associated as equals. These were invested with greater dignity, and they are placed at the head because they derive from on high and ascend for the benefit of the world and for the preservation of worlds. Similarly, the two lights ascended together with the same dignity. The Moon, however, was not at ease with the Sun and, in fact, each felt mortified by the other.

The Moon said, *"Where dost thou pasture?"* The Sun said, *"Where dost thou make thy flock to rest at noon? How can a little candle shine at midday?"* (Song of Songs) *God thereupon said to her (the Moon), "Go and diminish thyself."* She felt humiliated and said, *"Why should I be as one that veils herself,"* meaning to become diminished. Whereupon God said, *"Go thy way forth in the footsteps of the flock."* Whereupon she diminished herself so as to be the head of the lower ranks. From that time on, she has had no light of her own but derives her light from the Sun.

At first they were equal. Afterwards, she (the Moon) diminished herself among all those grades of hers, though she is still head of them. For a woman enjoys no honor save in conjunction with her husband.

89

It is important at this point to cite the recognition of astrology in the *Babylonian Talmud*, Tractate Hulin, pg. 60b:

> *Rabbi Shimon ben Pazi singled out a contradiction between several Biblical verses. One verse said, "And God made two great lights"* (Genesis 1:16) *and immediately the verse continues, "the greater light and the lesser light…"*

> *The Moon said to the Creator: "Is it possible for two kings to wear one crown? Can I and the Sun rule jointly over this vast universe?" And God responded, "Then go and make thyself smaller."*

> *"But Master of the universe," cried the Moon, "because I have suggested that which is proper, must I then make myself smaller?" To which God replied, "Go, and thou wilt rule by day and by night."*

> *"But what is the value of this?" bemoaned the Moon. "Of what use is a lamp in broad daylight?" God replied, "Go! The nation of Israel shall reckon by thee the days and the years."*

> *"But it is impossible," replied the Moon, "to do without the Sun for the reckoning of the seasons, as it is said: 'And let them be for signs and for seasons and for days and for years.'* (Genesis 1:14)*" And God continued, "Go! The righteous shall be named after thee. Inasmuch as you are made smaller, the righteous shall be called small."*

Thus we find Jacob the Small, (Amos 7:2) Saul the Small, (I Samuel 15:17) and others.

Upon seeing that it would not be consoled, the Holy One, blessed be He, said, "Bring an atonement for Me, for making the Moon smaller."

This beautiful and intriguing confrontation between the moon and God is the basis of an incredible *Zoharic* conclusion. Herein lies the secret of why Kabbalah uses the lunar-solar system to calculate the year as opposed to the solar system alone, which is the basis of the contemporary Western calendar. "And God said unto Abraham, 'Go out from your land and from your birthplace and from the house of your father.'" (*Genesis* 12:1) This command, according to the *Zohar*, told Abraham to leave the house of the moon, the house of Saturn, and the house of Mars, for when the house of Mars, the house of Saturn, and the moon rule it is said that one should never venture into some new undertaking, which also applies to the second day of the week, which is Monday, or the fourth day of the week, which is Wednesday. According to the *Zohar*, this is because Mars has the heat and redness of the Sun, and purgatory was created and brought forth on the second day of Creation. The astrological influence of Mars on that particular day is therefore one of extreme negativity. The original source of the energy that produced purgatory was of a negative quality.

The moon consists of both good and evil. When she is full, she is considered good, but in her waning stage, she is considered evil. Consequently, as an astral influence, she will shine negatively on the fourth day because on the fourth day, the moon reduced the energy field she was originally created with. As a result, the moon came to be known as impoverished, and in the time of her descent, negative energies pervade the universe.[22]

Of all the verses in the Bible, these particular passages in the *Talmud* and in the *Zohar* carry with them the entire idea of kabbalistic astrology, which is by far the most profound, most ancient, and most widely held concept in Kabbalah. These two passages reveal the whole system of astrology, and from them we can learn the very essence both of our universe and of the astral influences that completely envelop and, unfortunately at times, control the destiny of man. The implications of these passages are profound and sweeping. They demand a tremendous change in our present theories of astronomy and our concepts of the whole spectrum of astrology.

What emerges from the foregoing passages from the *Zohar* and the *Talmud* is the kabbalistic astrologer's view of the astral influence of planets and constellations, this view being very different from those held by contemporary astrologers. Sun-sign astrology is the extent of what most people consider to be all there is to know about astrology. A kabbalist, however, will tell you that analyzing sun signs is a long way from an in-depth astrological knowledge, inasmuch as external cosmic astral influences are simply manifestations and physical expressions of multi-changing forces and the resulting interactions of the relationships between them. This is over and above the compelling need to know the internal subatomic cosmic energy field of each celestial body that participates in this beautiful and magnificent cosmic production.

There is another point, stressed time and time again, which continues to elude many who seek in-depth energy patterns in their observation of the universe. From the kabbalistic viewpoint, behavioral patterns of celestial bodies are merely reflections of some internal cosmic intelligence that compels the particular celestial body to behave and move in its peculiar path.

When we ask why there is day and night or why there are 365 days in the year, the conventional answer is that the Earth has two main movements: It rotates on its axis, creating day and night by causing the sun to appear to move from east to west; and it makes a complete circuit of the sun in 365 days. The kabbalist's question, however, is not directed at the physical manifestation of either the Earth's rotation or its journey around the sun, but asks instead what peculiar cosmic intelligence force creates this particular physical expression of the Earth and its relationship with the sun. Why must there be a day and a night? Why does a gravitational force exist to assure the Earth's journey around the sun in the annual span of 365 days? Why does each season last approximately 91 days?

The reader of kabbalistic material must start to ask such questions because this new age of physics requires a completely new, revolutionary approach to the way in which we view the universe. The aspiring kabbalist must begin to ask this sort of question because to think in this fashion requires a new intellectual process and mandates a bit of rethinking.

Early kabbalists were familiar with the internal cosmic fields of celestial bodies and regarded observed movements across the Heavens as physical expressions of the interplay of cosmic extraterrestrial intelligence. They viewed each constellation and planet as an entity in which the constant forces of the four elements—water, fire, air, and earth—were operative. Their observations of the universe, drawn from the various reflections of the *Zohar*, enabled them to provide a valid guide for the individual in his search for a total understanding of self. Furthermore, and more importantly, they provided a discipline for human and moral behavior, taking the individual to a higher level of consciousness and consequently to a higher level of moral conduct.

The Sun and Moon exert the most direct influence over Earth's inhabitants, plus there are the astral influences of the main planetary bodies: Saturn, Jupiter, Mars, Venus, and Mercury. After passing these difficult obstacles, we find the whole of our universe amazingly simple and clear—so amazingly simple and clear that we will initially be prompted to ask, "Why have I never seen it that way?"

There never can be a better world until there are better people in it. When individuals reflect upon themselves and their own particular, unique misery, the important thing to consider is a better means for achieving major changes, including the alleviation of some of the basic problems that confront us all. The enlightenment presented earlier in this book was once reserved for a mere handful of sages, mystics, prophets, and holy people who, through reaching upper levels of cosmic consciousness while still in the flesh, could see man and the universe as they really are in all their beauty.

Unfortunately, science has all but done away with the value of the individual. Man now is part of a functioning unit. By compiling all the known facts and figures concerning man, we can then computerize him and extrude a model of behavior that excludes any personal uniqueness or identity. Progress reduces us to a numerical entity—a credit card that we take great care in preserving, at times even at the expense of our individual identity.

Through astrology, however, the individual becomes aware of his internal intelligent cosmic force. Only in astrology is there a recognition of the weak and strong characteristics that make up an individual. From Aries to Pisces, these ideas are generally known, and they provide the individual with a better tool with which he can discover himself. The internal knowledge of astrology, which was thought lost but was actually just concealed in the *Book of Formation*, stresses the point that whenever any movement in the music of the universe is noted, there is some internal metaphysical force that has brought it about to be sensed and, at times, actually seen.

In recounting the dialogue between the sun, the moon, and God, the *Zohar* makes the point that the reason the sun has less influence upon the moon when the moon begins to disappear is because the negative Left Column influence of the moon becomes more dominant following the 15th day of the new moon, bringing about the waning of the moon. Conversely, at the beginning of the new lunar month, we observe the moon in ascending waxing position, and what we experience then (and what the internal astral influence indicates) is the constant rise of the all-inclusive positive energy force, or the gradual revealment of this energy. This is the physical relationship between the sun and the moon.

It appears self-evident that the predictive nature of astral influences dictate the progression and environment of man. How, then, can we reconcile the concept that astrology is not fatalistic? How do we reconcile kabbalistic astrology with the destiny of man when that supposedly is in his own hands?

We find in the *Zohar*[23] a commentary on *Isaiah* 57:15: "I dwell in the high and holy places, yet also with him that is of a contrite and humble spirit, to revive the spirit of the humble and the heart of the contrite ones." Elsewhere, we find in *Psalms* 34:15: "Behold, the Lord is close to those of a broken heart and He saves those of a contrite spirit." These verses refer to those who are fellow-sufferers with the moon in her defect and regarding whom it is fitly said: "... to revive the heart of the contrite ones," that is, to make those who participate in the suffering of the moon also participate in the new life to be bestowed upon her in the.

future. Such sufferings undergone by these individuals are called "sufferings in a token of love," and prayer is the method by which the souls can be renewed with the renewal of each moon.

In short, while a fixed position is placed upon every individual, there still are choices he can make by which the element of distress can be removed. He can, if he wishes, transcend any position in which he finds himself by means of meditation and prayer. This is amplified in the *Zohar*[24]:

> *Hence Solomon, who knew everything, spoke thus: "I observe that all of the vast doings of the world are controlled by vast numbers of spirits, but the people of the world know not and regard not what it is that upholds them." (Ecclesiastes 1:8-11) Even Solomon, the wisest of men, could not comprehend them. He further states: "He has made everything good in its time; also He has set the mystery of the world in their heart, so that man cannot find out the works that God has made from the beginning to the end." (Ecclesiastes 3:11)*

> *Whatever the Creator has formed in the world has its own controlling grade that directs it either for good or for evil. There are grades of the Right and grades of the Left, and neither is evil unless it is out of balance with its counterpart. If a man goes to the Right, then whatever he does becomes a directing grade on that side. This helps him on and procures other helpers. But if he goes to the Left, then whatever act he commits becomes a directing force on that side. This in turn*

brings indictments against him while leading him further into that side.

Thus, whenever a man performs a good and proper act, the chieftain of the right side affords him help. This is indicative of the expression "good in its time," in which the act and its time become infinitely bound up together, and "he has set the mystery of the world in their heart," which means that the whole world and all its works depend solely on the will of man. Happy are those righteous ones who, by their good deeds, draw benefits upon themselves and upon the world. They know how to attach themselves to the grade called "time of peace." By virtue of their righteousness in the lower world, they influence the Upper World.

Thus it may be seen that everything in the universe is dependent upon man's free will. As it is written: "So that man cannot find out the works that God has done from the beginning, even to the end..." Inasmuch as it depends upon man's will whether his deeds are attached to the proper grade or to the improper one, the text continues: "I know that there is no good in them but to rejoice and to perform good actions so long as they live." (Ecclesiastes 3:12)

If a man's actions are not good, he has to rejoice at all of the consequences, however grim they may be. He should give thanks and do good actions as long as he lives. Even if his own acts have brought evil upon him through the grade that he himself initiated, he still must rejoice at the consequences and give thanks for them because he brought them on himself like a bird blindly falling into a snare.

Such consequences that are willingly, if unconsciously sought are for *tikkun* (correction) purposes and are therefore advantageous, even in pain. Self-pity, on the other hand, offers no advantage.

The *Zohar*[25] spells this out:

"For man also knows not his time; as the fishes that are taken in an evil net and the birds that are caught in a snare, even so are the sons of men snared in an evil time when it has fallen suddenly upon them." (Ecclesiastes 9:12)

The expression "in his time" refers to the ministering angel for that particular cosmic energy force called "time" who presides over each act a man performs. It is referred to in the statement: "He has made everything beautiful in its time." Hence they are "as the birds that are caught in the snare." Happy are those who exert themselves in the study of the Bible and are intimate with the ways and paths of the Bible and the Most High King so as to follow the true path.

The coded message we have received from the *Zohar* is that there are basically 28 astral periods of time: 14 good and 14 bad, or 14 positive and 14 negative times, throughout the year. The *Zohar* here is revealing the secret doctrine that these 14 times will move man with cosmic energy in the direction that man himself has chosen. If man's action is positive, he can direct the positive aspect at the very same time. If he moves in a negative direction, he then initiates what we might consider the button that activates the negative column. While the forces of cosmic energy and time do prevail and do control our universe, we nevertheless can draw from this *Zohar* the truth that man is still at the helm of the boat.

driving the bus.

And to man has been given this vast knowledge that had previously been concealed, even to King Solomon the Wise. This knowledge is revealed to us by the *Book of Formation* and by its subsequent profound commentary, the *Zohar*.

> *To everything there is a season and a time to every purpose under the Heavens. A time to be born and a time to die; a time to plant and a time to pluck up that which was planted. A time to kill and a time to heal; a time to break down and a time to build up. A time to weep and a time to laugh; a time to mourn and a time to dance. A time to cast away stones and a time to gather stones together; a time to embrace and a time to refrain from embracing. A time to get and a time to lose; a time to keep and a time to cast away. A time to rend and a time to sew; a time to keep silence and a time to speak. A time to love and a time to hate; a time of war and a time of peace. (Ecclesiastes 3:1-8)*

We have spoken of 28 astral influences: 14 on the positive side and 14 on the negative. These 28 "times" are all cited in the lovely passage above from Ecclesiastes.

These 28 times are energy forces that, from a kabbalistic viewpoint, can be intimately known and predicted so that we can be prepared to take advantage of them when they occur. They are cosmic energy centers just waiting to be put to good use. It is also noteworthy that all astral influences are based on the cosmic energy centers of the seven planets, which are related to the four basic elements of water, fire, air, and earth. And these seven planets, multiplied by the four elements of which they consist, again repeat the coded number: 28.

$$7 \times 4 = 28 = 10$$

*"IS THE UNIVERSE CREATED OR ETERNAL?
IT BEHOOVES US TO POINT OUT THE GREAT
DIFFICULTY OF THIS INVESTIGATION. FOR BY BEING
AWARE OF THE DIFFICULTY OF A PROBLEM,
WE ARE GUIDED TO THE WAY WHICH LEADS US
TO THAT ATTAINMENT OF THE TRUTH THEREOF."*

—Gersonides

CHAPTER FOUR

COSMIC WANDERERS

One cannot conclude a discussion of astral influences without paying due respect to that most mysterious and myth-laden celestial body of them all: The comet. For centuries, appearances of these solar wanderers have been greeted with awe, apprehension, and, as with so many other celestial phenomena, complete misunderstanding.

All that is certain, even today, about a comet is that it is a heavenly body consisting of a nucleus and a tail that extends to a vast length across the sky as it revolves around the Sun. Comets usually are distinguished from other members of the solar system by their diffuse appearance and the character of their orbits, which generally are elliptical and enormous. There are, however, some comets with orbits that so closely resemble those of some of the minor planets that any distinction becomes almost impossible. Since comets (with the exception of Halley's) appear at irregular intervals and move in a rapid and unpredictable fashion, they long have been regarded with mingled interest and fear.

Since mankind has long assumed that heavenly bodies exercise some control over the affairs of men, it is only natural that comets were once regarded with considerable suspicion and have been associated with omens of disaster, often foretelling the overthrow of kings and nations. The famed Bayeux tapestry portraying the Norman conquest of England in 1066 features Halley's Comet as a most terrifying object, but while it might have been an ill omen for the Saxon king who died at the Battle of Hastings with an arrow through his eye, it certainly bode no ill for William the Conqueror.

Comets are rebellious members of our solar system, appearing to obey none of the normal rules of the cosmic road. The planets all move in the same direction around the sun, while comets move with equal frequency in either direction. The orbits of the planets are nearly circular and lie very closely in the same plane. The orbit of a comet is very elongated and may lie along any plane.

Where comets originate remains a scientific mystery to this very day. Astronomers have postulated the Oort cloud, a hypothetical cloud of icy objects far beyond the orbit of Pluto, as the birthplace of comets, but little empirical evidence of this cloud's existence has been found. The scientific community prefers to avoid the ever-pressing kabbalistic question as to why comets appear at all because without a ready scientific answer, this question is always an embarrassment. The fact remains, however, that we probably know less about the origin of comets than about any other object in the cosmos. Theories postulated since man began to view the Heavens have shed little light upon the subject. Ideas of the mode or origin of comets are as numerous as the number of astronomers who have studied them.

Despite the fact that substantial progress has been made on the problem, definitive answers are not available. Generally accepted notions have had to be revised routinely in the light of new advanced technology relating to the frontiers of space, but convincing arguments have led to the rather commonly held conclusion that comets have always been members of our solar system, although data suggesting that they may have originated somewhere in the interstellar region of our universe are no longer rejected out of hand.

Since the mystery continues, once again we must advance the kabbalistic formula for a true understanding and ask "Why?" While available scientific evidence reflects upon and may ultimately have a bearing on comet origins, the kabbalistic method leaves little room for error.

Rather than starting from the present and working backward, as scientists do, the approach of Kabbalah is to begin at the beginning and proceed with the creative process down to the present. A good starting point for our investigation is the Hebrew word for comet. In the wisdom of Kabbalah, Hebrew letters and words are coded for the revelation of energy-intelligence. Consequently, the Hebrew name for "comet" should reveal its origin and intended energy-intelligence. Surprisingly enough, the Hebrew word, *shavit*, has an Aramaic counterpart, *sharvit*. For an interpretation of the significance of these similar words, let us turn to the *Zohar*[26].

> *Rav Isaac opened a discourse on the verse: "And the remnant of Jacob shall be in the midst of many peoples as dew from the Lord, as showers upon the grass that are not looked for from men, nor awaited at the bands of the sons of men." (Micah 5:6) "Observe," he said, "that every day, as soon as day breaks, a certain feminine [negative] cosmic force awaits her masculine mate for the cosmic connection to reveal the light of day that emanates from the Garden of Eden. Upon receiving the force of the Three-Column energy System, sharvit [shavit] rules as a scepter in maintaining balance in the universe."*

What seems to emerge from the *Zohar* is the mystery of the internal essence of a comet. It is the energy force of the Three-Column System whipping (*shavit*) the universe into shape. For this very reason, the Hebrew month of Aquarius is Shevat, indicating the advent of the Messiah along with its blessing of "peace on Earth and good will toward one's fellow man."

How is this all going to come about? The Bible, in *Numbers* 24:17, is very clear when it declares:

> *I see it, but not now shall it come to pass. I behold it, but it is not nigh. There shall come a star [the*

influence of the Zeir Anpin, the Three-Column System], and a scepter (shavit) shall rise out of Israel and shall smite the corners of Moab and destroy all the foundation thereof.

Coincidently, the numerical value of *Shevat* is 311, corresponding to the Hebrew word for *ish* (man).[27] The preceding verse points us to the concept surrounding the coming of the Messiah, as stated: "And now, behold, I shall go unto my people: Come therefore and I will advise thee what this people shall do to thy people at the end of days." (*Numbers* 24:14)

While the comprehension of the star of *shavit* was known to the kabbalists of the *Zohar*, the sages of the *Babylonian Talmud*, in Tractate Berachot pg. 58b were not as certain.

Rabbi Samuel said, "The orbits of the Heavens are known to me as the streets of my city Nahardaya. The star of shavit, however, is not understood."

Consequently, the kabbalistic interpretation of a comet is regarded as an omen of freedom and balance, rather than as an omen of disaster. The comet's tail represents the energy-intelligence of the *Vav* of the Tetragrammaton— *Yud, Hei, Vav,* and *Hei*—Holy Name of God. Therefore, its appearance is as a tail similar to the letter *Vav*, which portrays a rod or stick. The front round, or face, of the comet symbolizes the mating of *Malchut* with the *Vav* or the positive energy-intelligence of the *Vav*, with the negative energy-intelligence of *Malchut*, creating a unified circuit of energy. The effect of this mating is balance and stability.

The conclusion of what has just been said raises a serious question: Is the tail the result of the head or nucleus of the comet as it appears to us, or is it the other way around? From a kabbalistic point of view, the *Vav* precedes the last letter *Hei*, or *Malchut* (negative energy-intelligence), in its position in the Tetragrammaton. Thus, while the telescope or naked eye seems to observe the tail as being formed of molecules and dust particles driven out from the comet, indicating the comet came first and the tail second, kabbalistically, it is the other way around, just as the true influence of a comet, as perceived by mankind through the centuries, is the other way around.

Welcome the arrival of a comet. Potentially, it portends only the best!

*"TO SEE A WORLD IN A GRAIN OF SAND, AND
HEAVEN IN A WILD FLOWER; HOLD INFINITY IN THE
PALM OF YOUR HAND, AND ETERNITY IN AN HOUR."*

—William Blake, *Auguries of Innocence*

CHAPTER FIVE

BEYOND THE TEST TUBE

The dawn of true science, with the freedom to pursue open and honest inquiry into the cosmos, finally emerged after centuries of suffocating superstition and church dogma, when Nicholas Copernicus in 1543 proclaimed that the Earth and her sister planets revolved around the sun. Copernicus probably concluded his studies as early as 1530, but given the tenor of the times and the Church's predilection for consigning "heretics" to the Inquisitional bonfire, he prudently delayed publication until he was on his deathbed. Prior to Copernicus, the sun, moon, planets, and stars revolved around the Earth by papal decree, and to argue with that sort of proclamation was dangerous business.

Ironically, astrology now stands where Copernicus stood almost 500 years ago, while "pure" science joins modern religionists in the role of the 16th century Church. Science, ignoring the demands of its own methodology, not only scoffs at astrology's claims, but bluntly refuses even to examine them, while many of the Jewish faith still perceive astrology as something alien to Judaism. There are some Christians that even go so far as to brand astrology a work of Satan. As we can see, the concept of heresy unfortunately lives on, but as in Copernicus' day, its truth will succumb neither to threat nor to decree.

The study and practice of kabbalistic astrology should not be taken lightly, however. Its purpose goes far beyond the superficial "Hi there, what's your sign?" Kabbalistic astrology probes the very nature of reality. It points to a non-materialization of the space-time continuum and warns that the metaphysical unconscious really can cast a great deal of doubt on any hasty explanation of the parallels between the celestial and terrestrial universes, between the metaphysical astral influences of the world beyond and the physical world as we see it.

To fully assess astrological phenomena, one must take into account all the other phenomena with which we come into contact. In light of space exploration and other new dimensions, we can no longer ignore the existence of the metaphysical astral influence that astrology documents. Hopefully, through a little more clarification of the very basic *Talmudic* studies to which I have already referred, we can move ahead into the area of such phenomena, with the anticipation that astral intelligences will be very real and logical, if at times seemingly irrational. Kabbalistic astrology comes to grips with the unknown far more than physicists can, even with their new-found uncertainty principle.

Experimentation once was an attempt to study a system through analysis based on controlled stimulation. This exploration was followed by observation of the resulting response. Since the positing of the uncertainty principle, however, controlled experiments on a cosmic level can never accurately be determined. We have come to realize the role that theory and ideas play in the discovery of each new physical and cosmic phenomenon. Most cosmic phenomena have come to light only recently, principally through the introduction of new detection techniques into astronomy. It is only natural to wonder how much more remains unrecognized, given that technological advances have already uncovered so many new physical and cosmic features that one can only speculate about what further refinements may reveal.

The dilemma of observational experiments following the acceptance of the uncertainty principle has raised some grave doubts. Astronomy is fundamentally an observational science. Present technology is insufficiently advanced to permit physical exploration of the universe beyond our solar system. The distances that must be overcome are simply too enormous. Our most sophisticated robot probes become functionally useless the minute they cross the orbit of Pluto and plunge for aeons into the void that stretches between one tiny star in our galaxy and the next nearest one, and so vast is the distance to the next galaxy that physical travel across it may never even be attempted. Since the science of astronomy is so dependent upon observation, it is clear that the required technological advances are so complex as to verge upon the impossible.

In astronomy, the observer can choose either to detect and analyze signals from extraterrestrial sources or to simply ignore them. He has no way of provoking a cosmic source to change its emission. He can only observe that which is brought to his attention, relying on the information carriers such as satellites and radio telescopes that transmit all he will ever learn about the universe. These transmissions are infinite in nature. Most of the information currently known about extraterrestrial phenomena has been transferred to us by means of radio waves, infrared radiation, cosmic ray particles, and other vehicles so minute that they practically cease to exist in reality as we know it. For the present, no magic of technology can help us detect waves that never reach Earth. Science can only help the astronomer reach the known boundaries imposed by the physical universe itself. Thus, results of calculations by theoretical astrophysicists seem almost an exercise in futility, and there is already an uneasy feeling among leading scientists that long-range predictions on the progress of science are doomed to remain unrealized. And so the most enlightened scientists, unwilling however to confer legitimacy upon any study that ventures beyond materiality, lock themselves into the medieval absolutism that Copernicus fought against.

In 1902, a mere five years before he would become the first American scientist to win a Nobel Prize, in his book *Light Waves and Their Uses*, Albert A. Michelson wrote: "The more important fundamental laws and facts of physical sciences have all been discovered. These are now so firmly established that the possibility of their ever being supplanted in consequence of new discoveries is exceedingly remote."

Then, as today, most scientists were so confident of their own understanding of nature that they were usually unwilling to admit to the possibility of further revolutionary phenomena or startling discoveries, yet another example of how the scientific spirit resembles the dogma of religion. Walter Meissner, a colleague and student of the famous physicist and Nobel Prize winner, Max Planck, recalls the following story concerning young Planck's choice of his subsequent field of endeavor in preparation for entry into the University of Munich:

> "At first, he was uncertain whether to select classical philology, music, or physics," Meissner wrote. "He finally decided on physics; this in spite of the fact that the then professor of physics at the University of Munich, Phillip Jolly, advised him against it since (said Jolly) in the field of physics, there was nothing new to be discovered."
> —Walter Meissner and Max Planck, *The Man and His World*

Some 25 years later, Planck provided the approach to the quantum theory of physics. He was to set down the basic principles for investigative research of atomic and subatomic universes.

In conclusion, while the variety of observations we can undertake to explore is limited, the potential fields of observations (which seem to be concealed) are infinite. The behavior of the transmitters of information and the contents of the cosmic container together limit the scope of our observations. Where, therefore, can science or the astrophysicist go from here? One way to gain some perspective on the nature of cosmic phenomena is to read what the kabbalist has to say. His claim to the information as to how the cosmic universe got started in the first place is as close to its content as we might want to achieve.

The problem of the origin of the cosmos is truly baffling. One can imagine analyzing the seed of a tree, then upon seeing the tree itself, know that the secrets of a tree lie hidden within another, similar seed. The universe itself, however, does not furnish us with the seed or blueprint of our observable universe, so we must imagine some bootstrap process that began essentially with nothing. The *Sefer Yetzirah* (*Book of Formation*), along with its commentaries, does just that. We no longer have to content ourselves with a sense of wonder and awe of the Heavens. They provide us with answers as to the origin of cosmic life.

The restriction brought about the creative process, referred to by the kabbalist as the emanation of the ten essential energy-intelligences (*Sefirot*). This *restriction*—the Big Bang itself—at first became manifested as extraterrestrial thought energy-intelligences. "*Sof ma'aseh bemachshava tehila*" ("The final act first becomes manifest as thought"), declares famed Kabbalist Rav Shlomo Alkabetz. (*Lecha Dodi*, Shabbat Song)

Following the evaluation of the entire creative thought process, the thought process of the Big Bang subsequently became manifest as a material external entity, similar to the internal energy-intelligence that became enclothed within a corporeal body. *Tractate Nedarin* pg. 32a in the *Babylonian Talmud*, says to "put aside your foolishness... Israel is not under planetary influence." This does not affect the validity of astrology in its application to Abraham and Israel, but rather as it is applied to Israel as the retainer of the secrets of cosmic extraterrestrial intelligence. With proper use of astrology and its tools, Israel is not and never will be subject to these astral planetary influences. Does this imply the existence of an ability to alter cosmic influence at its source? Can man really act on matter in defiance of the fundamental principles of physics? Are there indeed separate laws that govern our universe: One, governing a universe where there is no room in the physical process for free will, and another in which the entire cosmos must comply with and is dependent upon the behavior of man? It has been suggested that quantum theory, with its involvement of the individual in its very essence, opens the door to the dependency of man's behavior. The accepted doctrine of a deterministic universe omitting the central figure of this multifaceted reality, seems to be swept away by the quantum factor. This is the matter with which the *Talmud* deals when it proclaims: "Israel is not under planetary influences."

One more source confirms this statement but unfortunately gives ammunition to those who would forbid the orthodox religious community to study astrology today.

To quote from the Babylonian *Talmud*, Tractate Pesahim pg. 113b:

> *Rabbi bar Hanah said in the name of Rabbi Samuel*
> *ben Marta, on the authority of Rabbi Josi of Hutzal,*
> *"How do you know that you must not consult*
> *astrologers? Because it is said, 'Thou shalt be*
> *wholehearted with the Lord.'"*

To add more weight to the argument that astrology in some way implies that we have no trust in the Creator, idol worshippers are referred to as worshippers of the stars, obviously indicating that anything connected in any way with astrology can be considered a display of disbelief in God and belief in the deification of the stars. Another major section that further strengthens the concept that astrology is something to be avoided can be found in a section of the Babylonian *Talmud, Tractate Shabbat* pg. 156a:

> *Rabbi Hanina said, "The planetary influence provides*
> *wisdom; the planetary influence also provides wealth.*
> *Israel is subject to astral influence." Rabbi Johanan*
> *said, "Israel is not subject to the constellations." Rabbi*
> *Johanan told how we know that Israel is not subject to*
> *planetary influence: "Because it is written, 'Thus says*
> *the Lord, learn not the ways and customs of the*
> *nations and be not dismayed at the signs of the*
> *Heavens for the nations are dismayed.' (Jeremiah*
> *10:2) They are dismayed, but not Israel."*

The position that Israel is not under planetary influence has become so grounded in orthodox culture that respectable leaders draw their own conclusions that astrology should be avoided, no matter how much evidence there might be to the contrary. Various other references, however, indicate that there are astral influences that all people, Israel included, are governed by. How long will we continue to reject astrology as one of the Creator's creations, made manifest on the fourth day of Creation when He declared that the larger light should rule by day and the lesser light by night? The religious position is similar to that of scientists who still hold the belief that our universe and all that it contains arose and developed by chance alone. The reason many accept this is because it provides a great deal of comfort to the individual and to others who do not want to be subject to a ruler, even if He rules the universe. In taking this sort of position, the individual really believes himself to be free but he will still be influenced by these celestial forces, however much he believes to the contrary. Astral influences are there, and like the law of gravity, they will not go away on the basis of disbelief. The religionist especially delights in debating the question of astrology because it can be turned into a Bible controversy. For the non-religious, who have been raised in a world where free will and free thinking are considered truth, the Bible is nothing more than a compilation of stories and ethical dimensions. This individual has been molded by Western science and Western philosophy, and while astrology is not foreign to him, he seldom looks beyond its superficial aspects. For the traditionalist, however, who still adheres to the old principles, we hopefully will provide some form of understanding, some logical insight, and show him that astrology is in opposition neither to science nor to religion.

In sharp contrast to the controversy among the rabbis as to whether or not Israel is subject to astral influences, several other readings from the *Zohar* and the *Talmud* provide clear illustration that astral influences do exist and that almost everything depends upon them. In the *Babylonian Talmud*, *Tractate Moed Katan*, Raba said, "Length of life, children, and sustenance do not depend on merit alone, but on *Mazal*, the constellation." The *Zohar*[28] states: "And Abram saw with his wisdom of the stars that he shall not have a son," and follows this with: "And the Lord asked Abram to go outside." (*Genesis*, 15:5) With this, God was doing more than merely calling Abram outside his home. He was telling him not to feel enslaved by the wisdom of the stars, saying "for you shall have a son." This tells us that Abraham did have knowledge of the stars. He knew the science of astrology but was told not to feel compelled by it.

Rav Akiva was told by astrologers that his daughter was destined to die on her wedding night. This precognition was a continuing source of pain up to and including the night of his daughter's marriage. Gloom and dread dominated the evening as friends and family waited for the inevitable to occur. But as his daughter entered the wedding hall, she removed her hat and hung it up by thrusting its pin into a wall separator prepared for the women. The evening passed without incident, and the guests left with gladdened hearts, saying that Satan had been thwarted. When the bride removed her hat from the wall, however, she noticed that the pin carried a drop of blood at its tip. Investigating the far side of the wall, she found a dead snake, its eye pierced by the pin she had thrust through the wall.

"What did you do to turn your destiny around?" her father asked her, and she replied, "A poor man came to the door in the evening during the ceremony and festivity. Everybody was busy at the banquet and there was no one to attend him, so I took the portion that was given to me and gave it to him."

"You have done a good deed," said Rav Akiva, "and you have been delivered from death; not only from an unnatural death, but from death itself."

This story shows that the knowledge of astrology from Abraham's time onward was widespread and widely accepted. Astrologers were obviously highly respected in the ancient community. What emerges from the story of Abram is the astrological prediction that he would never have a son with Sarai because of an active astral influence. But Abram, of course, did have a child with Sarai because of a name change (to be discussed in detail later) that altered his astrological chart and his spiritual DNA. In the case of Rav Akiva's daughter, death had been predicted, but was thwarted by her own action at the last minute. In both cases, a statement found repeated many times in the *Zohar* is affirmed: While the stars impel, they do not compel.

The *Zohar* states that Abraham was the first known astrologer. He knew the sciences of astrology and astronomy alike. It is to him that the authorship of *Sefer Yetzirah* is attributed, and it is at this point that we can separate Western scientific tradition from the kabbalistic view of the universe. From Newton's time on, the classical physicist felt he could, in principle, predict with absolute precision the evolution of the universe for all time to come. This mechanistic view failed to consider the role of mankind in the process. The same, however, might be said of astrology. In principle, there can be a prediction of universal evolution that is made with complete precision and absolute detail. But astrology from the kabbalistic perspective is also concerned with man's mortal accountability for his actions because the kabbalist knows that man's actions can alter the state of the universe. Man is not merely an observer who creates reality; he actually determines the ultimate results and thus has ultimate responsibility.

When physicists try to glimpse the universe at birth to see how primordial material evolved, they somehow impose their own view of reality, which theoretical physicist Werner Heisenberg aptly named the uncertainty principle. At Cern, (the European Organization for Nuclear Research) in Geneva, Switzerland, scientists hope to recreate conditions they *believe*—in the same sense that orthodox religionists "believe"—existed briefly after the explosive birth of the universe.

Particles forming the nuclei of all atoms are *believed* to consist of subatomic particles called quarks that are bound together by gluons. The latter, scientists *believe*, may not only form the glue that holds everything together, but may also be agents that bind together the nuclear particles themselves. This has led to *speculation* that under the extraordinary pressure and temperature that existed for a trillionth of a second after the Big Bang, the universe was formed entirely of freely moving quarks and gluons. Anticipating this revelation, physicists are attempting to recreate the conditions extant at the beginning of the universe by initiating the most powerful collisions of subatomic particles ever produced in a laboratory.

The least we can expect from such a wacky pursuit is their admission that this kind of hit-and-miss investigative approach is no more valid (and probably less so) than that of the kabbalist, who asserts that he not only knows the exact condition extant at the time of the Big Bang but that he also understands the cause and motivation that brought the Big Bang into existence.

Despite probing by generations of physicists, insight into the internal workings of the atomic nucleus is still imperfectly understood—and will undoubtedly remain so until such time as science begins to view nature from a fresh perspective. The kabbalistic view of the universe, which proposes that mankind is not only a participant but also a determinator of all energy activity, involves radical changes in the traditional concepts of space and time.

At one time, even in recent memory, technology was regarded as the unlimited problem-solver, and progress was considered the cure for all of man's ills. By rejecting outright man's position and importance within the cosmos, science has caused a significant shift in the value system adopted by large segments of the general population from one of inner personal development to one of economic and technological concerns.

The principles of Newtonian physics still maintain a strong influence on Western scientific thinking, as many scientists continue to cling to this outdated mechanistic paradigm in spite of quantum theory, which posits the intimate relationship between human consciousness and the physical world.

Consequently, seeking the path of least resistance while still having to admit to man's participation in the establishment of reality, they stop short of the kabbalistic concept that mankind's role within the universe might also be that of a determinator.

From the kabbalistic point of view, the universe exists in a definitive and never-changing state. Change is a condition experienced only in the physical world. The real world is eternal and infinitely still. According to kabbalah, 99 percent of what we normally perceive as reality is an illusion. The illusion is composed of all of life's uncertainties, fragmentations, and all that changes—in short, everything that has to do with the physical world—whereas reality never changes.

The world of matter must comply with the illusionary laws of physics, which on the macroscopic level (ignoring quantum) are mechanical and deterministic. These laws seem to appear incompatible with free will.

Can the consciousness somehow reach into the physical world and create changes in defiance of the fundamental principles of physics? No, says the kabbalist.

One has merely to reflect on human activity to suspect that some mad metaphysical scientist is on the loose. In fact, according to Kabbalah, the tumult of physical existence was actually placed on Earth for the specific purpose of allowing man free will sufficient to alleviate Bread of Shame. This concept of relative free will can assist us in transcending the notion of personal isolation and can give amazing insights into our intimate connection with the all-embracing cosmos. It is this unity to which the kabbalist aspires.

The ability to change destiny through what we know as human free will does not necessarily contradict the mechanistic world view of our universe. The trick is to reach another dimension and change what might have been a predictable picture. Once we achieve an altered state of consciousness, the predictability of the mechanistic view of our universe no longer applies.

Actually, this is not as esoteric as it may sound. The phenomenon of the black hole, a collapsed star so dense and so powerful in its gravitational pull that not even light can escape it, is an example of an altered state of physical consciousness. DNA, the physical blueprint of everything that lives, is another. We shall examine both, then attempt to apply their principles to the nonmaterial, metaphysical alteration of consciousness that the kabbalist seeks as a means of changing what might appear to be an immutable destiny. Just as the astronomer probes a black hole with various radio waves to learn more about its structure and just as the geneticist performs surgery on genes to alter the creature they are designed to produce, the kabbalist uses prayer, meditation, and often little more than a change of name to alter his astrological chart and with it, his destiny. The scientist journeys through space, interstellar or interatomic to achieve his purpose. The kabbalist journeys through time.

Black holes represent for the physicist the ultimate unknown—and possibly the unknowable—in science. They constitute an edge or boundary of space-time where matter and cosmic influences enter or leave the physical universe in a totally unpredictable manner. Some cosmologists believe the universe emerged, without cause, from just such a primeval naked singularity, which is the closest concept science has found to a paranormal entity.

Even the practitioners of quantum mechanics have finally agreed that our knowledge, even of the inanimate elements of the world, cannot provide a complete picture. Nature operates in ways not fully deterministic, always tantalizing the observer with the suspicion that something is missing. The most we can predict about any physical system is the probability of its evolving in a variety of ways, but never in the determining view can we predict the evolution of a system in time. The uncertainty principle has reduced the possibility of knowing all of the universe to little more than an educated guess.

What an astrological chart can predict at one level, however, can be altered by man's moral actions, as is stated in the *Zohar*. Through astrology, we literally see the moral accountability of man for his actions, as reflected in the movement of the stars themselves. The following passage from the *Zohar*[29], which emphasizes again that while the stars impel, they do not compel, illustrates this point:

> *Over all the stars and constellations of the firmament, there have been set chiefs, leaders, and ministers whose duty is to serve the world, each one according to his appointed station. And even the tiniest blade of grass on Earth has its own appointed star in Heaven. Each star, too, has over it a being appointed who ministers before God as its representative, each according to its order. Each and every single star in the firmament keeps vigil over this world. They are appointed to minister to every single object in this world, for to each star there is a peculiar and particular object.*

As bizarre and incredible as this Zoharic interpretation of the existence of the stars may sound to the scientific community, the *Zohar* presents in it a clear purpose associated with celestial bodies. To the author of the *Zohar*, the central issue is not the examination of a massive star nearing the end of its life to form a black hole. The question addressed by Kabbalah in general and the *Zohar* in particular is how and why it all began. The kabbalist declares that stars provide such an inexhaustible supply of energy that they can sustain even as small a physical entity as a blade of grass. Celestial bodies are the mechanism by which metaphysical, primordial energy, which is the totality of an intelligence, becomes manifest. What, then, can be stated with regard to the state of our cosmology that preceded the appearance and manifestation of the galaxies? From what the *Zohar* has declared, it is clear that the pre-galactic period consisted of un-manifested, infinite numbers of intelligences that became the metaphysical seeds for future manifestation and evolvement. It is the sphere of the absolute, where opposing extremes of energy force intelligences merge and become reconciled.

Is this concept any different from that attributed to DNA and proven in laboratory tests? DNA, too, is the repository of enormous, almost infinite variations of future manifestations crammed into a volume so minute that it can be seen only through a powerful microscope. From uncountable seeds of uncountable galaxies to infinite seeds of infinite DNA manifestations, the great *Zoharic*[30] truth is demonstrated: "As above, so below." We may once again paraphrase it to say: "As in the metaphysical, so in the physical."

In the metaphysical universe, stars do not shine constantly, transferring energy without cessation. Rather, they are radiant only at appointed intervals. The *Zohar*[31] continues:

> *As soon as their purpose is fulfilled they (each unit of consciousness, or intelligence) are seen no more in this world, but they ascend to their appointed places above.*

Thus, our mundane universe and our own physical bodies both reflect and point to the constant back-and-forth movement between basic reality and the reality of the Upper Celestial Systems that constitute the timeless, spaceless realm we must reach if we are to be true masters of our own destiny. To illustrate this point further, let us reflect for a moment on the response of an atom to outside stimulation. In an atom, some of the electrons when stimulated become excited and respond by moving into a higher orbit, further away from the nucleus. Remove the stimulation and they drop back into their former orbital shells. Infinite changes and emissions of various types of energies almost certainly take place in the process.

A similar process occurs in our physical bodies. Physical or emotional stimulation of our bodies or psyches elicits different responses, some subtle, some more apparent. Penetration and observation of deeper, microscopic areas, lets us see the rapid back-and-forth movements that take place in this process. Metaphysically, some of these movements will even exceed the speed of light at higher orbital levels where the internal intelligences of all DNA are revealed.

Unfortunately, for the present at least, there is no way of knowing whether this rapid movement beyond the speed of light actually exists since we have no instruments capable of detecting or measuring it. But the activity, postulated on the metaphysical plane, might very well be the underlying cause of psychic disorders that constantly baffle our psychiatrists. What seems to emerge from the *Zohar* is the matter-of-fact declaration that when stimulation is removed from celestial entities, they react precisely in the fashion of entities on the mundane plane by retiring to their former positions. They in effect go back in time (repudiating Einstein's limiting concept of light speed as an absolute) to await the next stimulation or purpose that will assign them a functional, manifested program within the total cosmic design. This process, involving entities that truly are intelligences, varies in no way from the internal, pre-programmed function of DNA.

Thus, seemingly far-out proposals about the universe as described in Kabbalah become socially acceptable. After all, how and where did this highly intelligent double helix called DNA originate? DNA is a highly sophisticated computer that defies the imagination of any computer scientist, and it must be considered highly likely that after the transition period called death, the higher intelligence forms, of which DNA is only one, continue their existence on levels above the physical. Who can deny that intelligent energy forces go back in time to their former positions, just as electrons do when a stimulus is removed? Does it not follow, therefore, that they will return again to the physical plane when the proper stimulus—in this case, rebirth through reincarnation—is resumed?

What, then, are these intelligences that occupy both the physical and metaphysical worlds and are capable of moving back and forth between them? Simply stated, they are the direct result of the Desire to Receive, which is the root of all forms of intelligence. When describing the evolution of matter, we are really discussing the evolution of consciousness of the Desire to Receive. In his book *An Entrance to the Zohar*, Rav Ashlag explains that this desire is in itself a form of intelligence that is little more than a synonym for consciousness, and it consists of the four primary aspects of reality in their unmanifested form, which in the absolute had its origin within the Endless Realm (*Ein Sof*). When stimulated with purpose, these four intelligences become the basis of all subsequent manifested physical matter, which in turn ultimately becomes some life form entity of manifest energy. All the infinite forms of intelligences that crowd our galaxy and others have their origins within the Endless and account for every life form we can observe.

In his volume called *Tree of Life*, Rav Isaac Luria (the Ari) states:

> *There are four basic realities of intelligence or thought in our mundane universe, namely, the inanimate reality, vegetation reality, animal reality, and human reality. These four realities are extensions of the four basic elements of fire, air, water, and earth. These four elements are in turn an extended manifestation of the four primal, basic intelligences of the Desire to Receive, known as the four stimulations of Chesed (Mercy), Gevurah (Judgment), Tiferet (Beauty) and Malchut (Kingdom).*

What is the fundamental difference in character between these four realities? Let us begin our investigation with the lowest reality: The inanimate. Why does the Ari consider the inanimate kingdom the lowest reality? Ever since mankind entered the new age of subatomic physics, we have begun to understand the enormous activity that takes place within a rock. This energy, contained by all matter, is, according to the Ari, an extension and manifestation of one of the aspects of intelligence (stimulus) of the Desire to Receive. As we penetrate the reality of matter, we find the smallest and weakest amount of power, desire, stimulation, and intelligence of the four realities. A rock does not have the ability either to bring near that which benefits it or to push away that which is harmful. Thus, its level of intelligence and consciousness is the least of all the realities.

The desire or intelligence of the vegetative species, while similar in this respect to animal and human reality, still does not possess an individuality of consciousness. Its power of desire to reject that which is harmful and to accept that which is beneficial is common to every species of the plant kingdom, but that intelligence stimulates and makes manifest only the physical expression of immobility. It cannot, by and within itself, possess the mobility inherent in human and animal realities, yet plants, unlike rocks, do react physically to the stimuli of sunlight, water, heat, and cold.

The animal reality is on a higher level of consciousness. Its Desire to Receive is more intense, and its stimulation, or internal energy force, possesses its own individual sense of selection in rejection or acceptance of that which is either harmful or beneficial. Its internal intensity provides for a broader freedom of movement in three dimensions. The freedom of movement seen in the animal kingdom is a direct result of the internal consciousness level already included within its DNA complex. The level of the Desire to Receive implanted within the DNA of the plant kingdom is the primal cause of the manner in which its physical manifestation evolved; plants do not walk or talk or move in three dimensions because their level of consciousness is of a lower intensity.

The supreme and most intensified Desire to Receive belongs to the human reality. We are humans simply because our primal cause of activity and higher levels of consciousness include the power to reason and to articulate speech—a gift enjoyed by no other species on Earth. Once manifested, it produced a DNA that permitted the physical expression and evolvement of intensified activity. The human reality is not limited by space or time. This intelligent life form has the ability to think about any other reality wherever it may be in our universe. The higher level of consciousness permits man to think even about those who died generations ago and of those yet unborn in the future.

This reality indicates a mobility of the psyche as well as of the body. Thus the concept of expanded consciousness belongs exclusively to the realm of the human reality, which relates to and can initiate the interpenetration of its DNA by the level of its Desire to Receive. Our physical bodies are the ultimate manifestation, end products, and result of these higher intelligences that originated within the Endless. Inasmuch as the human reality is not limited by space or time, we *Homo sapiens* have the capability to travel back into time, faster than the speed of light. The *Zohar* has already declared that one can find within man the exact system that exists in the Celestial Realm. We may experience the more subtle levels of people and objects, including the interrelationships between people, as energy transfers interact between them. In this state, the structure of the cosmos opens up to us and shows us its past, present, and future, all in a single instant that springs free of the space-time continuum.

What seems to emerge from all this is the direct relationship that exists between the four realities and their constant interaction on the most subtle levels. Most important is man's connection to and interplay with the cosmic presence. When the kabbalist speaks with such assurance and delivers his crystal-clear interpretation of the cosmic world, he speaks with authority because he has travelled this faster-than-light speed route. He has returned to and observed the state from whence all cosmic presence evolved. By this means, primal instant communication is possible all across our galaxy and into other galaxies as well.

These four realities must be understood if the kabbalistic method of examination itself is to be understood. Without this understanding, the kabbalistic rejection of the common concept that the stars shine at all times but only reveal themselves to us at night would seem to border upon madness. The kabbalist, however, knows that things do not happen merely on the physical level. All things are directed by an internal energy force of intelligence that interpenetrates particular celestial bodies and evolves into that which we observe in manifest form. The findings of astronomy, confined as they are to the physical realm, have little bearing on the matter.

An example of the human reality transcending the frame of space-time may be seen in the following experiences of Moses in *Deuteronomy* 32:48-49:

> *And the Lord spoke to Moses that same day, saying, "Go up into this Mount Avarim, to Mount Nebo, which is in the land of Moab, to the top of Pisga, facing Jericho; and behold the land of Caanan, which I give to the children of Israel for a possession."*

> *And Moses went up from the plains of Moab to the mountain of Nevo, to the top of Pisga, facing Jericho. And the Lord showed him all the land of Gilead, to Dan, and all Naphtali, and the land of Ephraim, and Manasseh, and all the land of Judah, as far as the utmost sea and the Negev, and the plain; the valley of Jericho, city of the palm trees, as far as Zo'ar. And the Lord said to him, "This is the land which I swore to Abraham, to Isaac and to Jacob, saying, 'I will give it to thy seed.'"* (Deuteronomy 34:1)

> *For Moses already knew at this time that he was not to enter the land, and since he wanted to know of it before he departed, he sent the spies. When they failed to bring him back a proper report, he did not send again, but waited till the Lord showed him the land.*[32]

Not only did Moses view the entire land, which was possible only because of his expanding consciousness that permitted him to see the entire breadth and length of Israel from this one vantage point, but in addition, he was shown all future leaders of each generation to come.

The relationship between theory and observation is understandably complex. Without observations, theory can only suggest the possibilities, and the uncertainty in prediction of knowledge is something very certain.

Theory, observation, and the scientific method provide the framework for conceiving and understanding that which has been observed. Observation by itself does not provide the facts required for understanding. When astronomers found new stars and gave them names, only the astrophysicist could associate the incoming energy forces and radiation with these celestial bodies. Actual experience in science, however, seems to add a great deal more confusion to what is really going on than scientific definitions are able to clarify. More often than not, the assumptions and conclusions of science lead into a blind alley. Science is a human undertaking by dedicated humans who, for all their advanced techniques, are subject to mistakes.

The major shortcoming in the area of cosmology lies in the distance that separates man from his cosmos. The untouchables continue to elude the posse of scientists so bent on their capture. Despite the power of the human mind to perceive, sort out, and choose from the wealth of information and data provided by space exploration, the mysterious world of outer space continues its flight to the unknown. There can be no marriage between earthlings and the vivid intelligences out there. Their space secrets represent an eternal veil drawn across the universe, cloaking it in utmost secrecy and giving rise to the words of the Psalmist: "The heavens declare the glory of the Creator, the expanse of the sky tells of His handiwork." (*Psalms* 19:2) The Heavens have by no means yielded up all their mysteries, and even as new technological systems are developed, the universe will meet them with new challenges within the frontiers of science.

The *Zohar* transcends science, and when such a comprehensive work appears in the Age of Aquarius, much speculation on the origin of the planets, their cosmic intelligence, and their specific purpose in the scheme of things can finally be laid to rest. The *Zohar* not only raises questions we never dared ask, but to receive answers to these questions, the *Zohar* is the source we must go to. Let us examine some of the phenomena it presents.

Do stars shine all day long, even though we cannot see them when they are bathed in sunlight? The scientist will assure us that they do, but the *Zohar* says they do not. Herbs, trees, and plants cannot grow and flourish save under the influence of the stars that watch over them from above and gaze upon them face to face, each according to its own particular astral influence.

Most planets, stars, and constellations appear at the beginning of each evening. They usually remain for three hours, less a quarter. From that point on, stars with lesser astral influences appear. However, these lesser stars do not shine or influence in vain. They are conducting and influencing and exercising their own peculiar magnetic fields the entire night to enable flowers and plants to grow and blossom.

Then there are those planetary bodies that serve until midnight strikes, performing their particular duties and transferring their own particular magnetic fields until the appointed hour that they have been ministered to share. There are planetary entities that serve the universe for a very short period in the evening. They appear only as long as the blade of grass takes to receive its total sustenance; there is then no further need for these entities to continue ministering their cosmic energies. But no planetary entity stands in vain. As soon as each has finished and has completed its cosmic endeavor, it returns to its appointed place, no longer appearing in this world.

In the book of the higher wisdom of the East, we learn about the peculiar planetary bodies called comets. A comet is a particular star that forms a tail, or a scepter, in the firmament. There are certain herbs in our universe, the kind called "elixirs of life," that receive their cosmic influence and energy from comets. In addition, their cosmic magnetic fields transfer this energy and produce precious stones and fine gold, which form within the breast of high mountains under shallow water, and which are ruled by the particular comet under whose influence they grow and increase.

The cosmic energy of the comet is provided by a mere glance its luminous tail that trails across the sky and that causes those things to flourish.

Certain illnesses of man, as jaundice, can be cured through the patient's gazing upon shining steel, which is held before his eyes and rapidly moved from side to side so that like a comet's tail, it sends flashes of light into the face, thus healing the disease. Therefore all those objects over which such stars as these are appointed can have no proper development and growth unless the light of the comet actually passes over them. They are then enabled to renew their color and their energy according to their need. It is similarly indicated in the Book of King Solomon, in regard to the science of precious stones, that when these stones are denied the light and sparkle of certain stars, their development is retarded and they never reach their full perfection. God has ordered all things so that the world may be perfected and beautified. Accordingly, it is written that the stars are "to give light upon Earth" (Genesis 1:17) in all the things which the world needs for its perfection.[33]

I cannot say for certain that the cosmic traveler referred to in the *Zohar* is Halley's Comet. What seems to emerge from the *Zohar's* explanation of the comet (*sharvit*) is that this cosmic traveler is more than merely some sort of celestial spectacle. Comets are fundamentally cosmic energy capsules. The shining tail that produces a beautiful evening star streaming halfway across the sky is definitely more than merely a sight to observe.

"WHAT'S IN A NAME? A ROSE BY ANY OTHER NAME, WOULD SMELL AS SWEET."

—William Shakespeare

CHAPTER SIX

WHAT'S IN A NAME?

illiam Shakespeare wrote some beautiful poetry, but had he been a student of Kabbalah, he would have come up with a different answer to Romeo's plaintive question: What's in a name? Everything is in a name. A name is the linchpin of control, the dividing line between blind destiny and free will. Witness Adam's first assigned task in the Garden of Eden:

> *And out of the ground the Lord God formed every beast of the field and every fowl of the air and brought them unto Adam to see what he would call them, and whatsoever Adam called every living creature, that was the name thereof.* (*Genesis* 2:19)

This exercise was designed to do far more than keep Adam occupied and insulate him from *ennui*. Of all the fears that bedevil mankind, none is so terrifying as the fear of the unknown because what is unknown can neither be avoided nor controlled. Which warning would you rather hear whispered on a dark night: "A tiger is out there" or "Something is out there"? Which strikes the greater chill?

By naming the creatures of a newly formed world, Adam became the master of his environment, but he was not the last of his line to wield the power of a name. Generations later, guided by the hand of God, a man named Abram was to refine the naming art in a manner calculated to change the history of the world.

Again from *Genesis* 12:1-3:

> *Now the Lord said unto Abram, "Get you out of your country and from your kindred and from your father's house unto the land that I will show you. And I will make you a great nation and I will bless you and make your name great; and you shall be a blessing. I will bless them that bless you, and him that curses you I will curse. In you shall all the families of the Earth be blessed."*

The Bible continues in *Genesis* 12:7:

> *And the Lord appeared to Abram and said, "Unto your seed I will give this land."*

The promise was a heady one, but Abram, who was wise in the ways of the Chaldeans and an adept in the science of astrology, had reason for skepticism. His wife, Sarai, was barren. Abram had no seed to receive the land offered and he saw in the stars, as if carved in stone, that he was destined to die childless, leaving all his worldly goods to distant relatives.

> *And Abram said, "Behold, to me You have given no seed, and the one born in my house is my heir." And, behold, the word of the Lord came unto him saying, "This man shall not be your heir, but he that shall come forth out of your own body shall be your heir."* (*Genesis* 15:3-4)

Then, in a process that would turn the skeptic into a man of such faith that he later would prepare, without question, to sacrifice his only son at a holy command, God revealed to Abram the metaphysical mechanism by which he might rewrite the destiny he had seen for himself in the stars. Abram, at the command of God, added the Hebrew letter *Hei* both to his name, changing Abram to "Abraham," and to the name of his wife, Sarai, changing her name to "Sarah." By this process, they seized the reins of destiny and changed their stars in an act of free will. *Hei*

> *And the Lord brought him [Abram] outside and said: "Look now toward Heaven and count the stars, if you are able to count them." And He said unto him, "So shall your seed be." And he believed in the Lord and He counted it to him for righteousness.* (*Genesis* 15:5-6)

As with everything in the coded text that is the Bible, the central message is packaged with several others, and before we delve into the meta-mechanics of the horoscope—

altering a name—it may be well to examine a few of them. The dialogue between God and Abram would seem to indicate a normal conversation between two individuals, almost as if both were conversing in Abram's home. After making the promise "he that comes forth out of your own body shall be your heir," the Lord takes Abram "outside." What, however, is "outside" or "inside" to God? As the Creator, He is all-pervading and omnipresent—the all-inclusive Positive Energy discussed in detail in my book *Kabbalah for the Layman*. This shift from metaphysical reality to the metaphor of the physical plane introduced the anthropomorphic God that all the great religions have since been based on.

The impersonal Lord, a pure Energy devoid of physical form or substance, is one that few people can connect or feel affinity with. But when the Creator was cast in something approaching human form, it became incumbent upon all subsequent believers to recognize His presence as all-pervading, whether or not they understood the kabbalistic maxim of that which is to be revealed must first be concealed. The concealment of total spirit in an anthropomorphic image in order to reveal it to mankind was the factor designed to eventually end war, hatred, greed, and envy. The fact that such a blissful state of harmony never materialized certainly does no credit to existing religions.

Still, when the word "Lord" appears in the Bible as a personal, intimate concept, the possibility of our connecting and creating an affinity with the Creator becomes enormously enhanced. Thus, when the kabbalistic decoding of the word "Lord" indicates an all-pervading intelligent force present in everything in and around us, connection becomes self-realized, with our personal makeup and psyche eternally bound up and connected with it. It is then only logical to decide that we had best learn what this intelligent force is all about and what makes it tick, and more importantly, to become very careful not to behave in a way that might cause the energy flow process to be disturbed. In short, if stealing, hating, envying, and making war are obstacles to being a functional creature, then we should give second thoughts to any temptation to embark upon such a course of negativity. Crime, in the long run, really does not pay. Perceived liabilities vastly outweigh any short-term gain.

Seen in this light, no human soul would be so foolish as to antagonize this internal intelligent force (the spark of the God within each of us) or invite its wrath. No one can fool an intelligence. Our own internal energy, not some outside force, is at stake here, and this internal energy is very important because it is the force that permits growth and movement without which the individual is dead.

This resolved, let us return to the vital dialogue between Abram and a suddenly corporeal Lord. What does His request that Abram go outside and count the stars mean, and what is its connection with the preceding verse that states: "This man shall not be your heir, but he that has come forth out of your own body shall be your heir"? Was it necessary for God to prove His point by telling Abram to count the stars or was the order given to shore up Abram's wavering faith?

In *Genesis* 15:6, "Abram believed in God and He counted it to him as righteousness," but is Abram really to be commended for believing, after having been told that just as he cannot count the stars, so shall be his seed? Believing is not a concept in the lexicon of Kabbalah. When we say, "I believe," we are instantly declaring our disbelief. Only when we say, "I know," do we erase all doubt. But Abram had to be made to understand that he had to grasp a higher level of consciousness if he was to accept God's bounty. He could not remain in the lower parallel state where a son could not be born. He would have to leave the lower level where he was known in the stars as Abram and rise to the level of *Koh* where he would be known as Abraham in the metaphysical realm that the internal cosmic influences of celestial bodies pervade. *Koh* indicates the Holy Name that was linked to him on the higher levels of consciousness. It is the gateway of prayer through which man obtains his requests.

When the Creator added the letter *Hei* to the names of both Abram and Sarai, He said, "Neither shall your name any more be called Abram, but you shall be Abraham, for the father of a multitude of nations (*av hamon*) have I made you." (*Genesis* 17:5) Here, God actually was creating an acronym from two words, av and *hamon*, meaning literally "father of a multitude of nations." The previous name, Abram, meant simply "father of Aram," which is the place Abram/Abraham came from.

God then told Abraham to cast new horoscopes and prepare new natal charts for himself and his wife, using the name changes as the new moment of birth for each of them.

Abraham thus was raised to a new level of consciousness and given an entirely new set of planetary influences, altering the destiny that said he would never father a child. It was this act that gave rise to the tradition that Israel is not governed by the stars.

We can now comprehend the importance of the different levels of consciousness that we can achieve and use to literally alter our destiny. Man does, in effect, create his own destiny, and this fact is not in conflict with his astrological natal chart. The chart of a destiny may be predicted but because the stars impel and do not compel destiny can be changed.

To this day, an old Orthodox Jewish tradition is to change the name of a person who is gravely ill, with an eye toward changing the person's destiny of death. This spiritual practice is a tool we use at The Kabbalah Centre. We emphasize the importance of names and changes of names because we understand that names are much more than simple labels by which we identify ourselves. From a kabbalistic point of view, names relate to the metaphysical, non-limiting aspect of space and time and become a channel for metaphysical transfers of energy. Biblical names can draw positive energy to a person, thus when a person is ill we participate in a meditative process to redirect the energy of their name for their benefit. Strange as this practice may seem in this technological age, many people will testify that the rebirth accompanying a name change, and the new natal chart that results, has improved their well-being.

It is well established that the changing of a name elevates the individual to a higher level of consciousness. Christian clerics who enter holy orders have followed this practice for years, frequently assuming a biblical name or a name sacred to their doctrine. This does not mean, however, that all we have to do is proclaim a new name for our self (or get the civil courts to proclaim one for us). There is no spiritual validity to the court process, and before any name change can have the desired effect, we must first strive to change our Desire to Receive for the Self Alone to a Desire to Receive for the Sake of Sharing.

Whatever the process required and whatever the method instituted, however, the *Zohar* gives clear indication of the validity of astrology and the absolute influence that celestial bodies manifest upon the universe, and, more importantly, that we can change the destiny that was programmed for us. Abraham changed his name and removed himself from his original natal astrological influences, but he did more than that: He changed his address as well. Remember that in *Genesis* 12:1, "the Lord said unto Abram, 'Get you out of your country and from your kindred and from your father's house to the land that I will show you....'" What seems to be indicated here by rabbinical sources, including the *Zohar*, is the expression "Meshaneh makom, meshaneh *mazal*," which means that when one changes the place where he lives, he also will also induce a metaphysical change in his personal constellation.

All of us come into life facing things we cannot control, yet life does seem to be a curious amalgam of inexorable fate and free will. Contrary to the highest precept of democracy, all men are not created equal. Through reincarnation and the *tikkun* (correction) process, humanity is created with a multitude of handicaps, burdens, and travails, and overcoming these is another process entirely.

As dealt with in detail in my book *Kabbalah for the Layman*, the universe began under the law of cause and effect, which corresponds with the biblical verse: "Whatever a man sows, that also shall he reap; they that plow iniquity and sow wickedness reap the same." (*Job* 4:8) This translates directly to the metaphysical law of *tikkun*, which is parallel to the Newtonian law of physics that states, "for every action, there is an equal and opposite reaction." When both are observed at the mundane level, the only difference between the universal law of *tikkun* and the physical law of action and reaction is the scope of each one. With the advent of Einsteinian physics, came a clue as to how we can reconcile both aspects of the same universal whole. Cause and effect, on one level, will produce everything according to the universal law of cause and effect. Other elements, however, can alter the entire existence and composition of the very same thing.

Astrology is a science that provides us with predictable information coinciding with the aspect of fate along the lines of Newtonian classical physics. When we consider the aspect of achieving another level of consciousness, we are not rejecting science, we are merely taking in the broader spectrum of things extant at the more subtle, subatomic level to alter the same universal law of cause and effect.

Each must be applied on a different level. The law of *tikkun* is a continuous experience, and as long as *tikkun* is not achieved because of a life stipulated by prior incarnations, we can safely state that the universal law of cause and effect has come into play and there is little one can do to alter it at that level.

Once we have ascended the spiritual ladder, which is the key to achieving *tikkun* and correcting the faults and flaws of prior incarnations, we have altered the state of the flaw and by so doing, changed that parallel level of consciousness that dictates the path we will take throughout our lifetime. This achievement permits us to elevate to another level of consciousness by the process of *tikkun*. What this means, in fact, is that we have repaired the original flaw that brought the expected metaphysical DNA pattern into our life. In effect, what we are considering when discussing parallel levels or altered states of consciousness is a literal move from one metaphysical DNA level pattern to another.

It is not my intent at this point to present a case for the authenticity or validity of reincarnation. That ground has already been covered in my book *Wheels of a Soul*. The point I want to make here is simply to emphasize that knowledge of astrology enables the individual to provide a rational explanation of life and its mysteries based on the ascertainable law of cause and effect. The metaphysical DNA is merely a printout of our previous lifetimes. Based on our past behavior both positive and negative—the infinite actions—a new, reborn, metaphysical DNA is created as an embodiment of all our prior actions. The interface between the physical and metaphysical realms, between the present and composite metaphysical DNA, is the lineup of the astral bodies at the time of our birth.

The kabbalistic view of astrology, however, is dramatically different from the conventional pursuit of this science. Conventional astrology contends that the individual will take a course of action because of the arrangement of the stars, whereas Kabbalah maintains that the *tikkun* process puts the individual in an astrological position so that the stars will impel him in the needed direction. Are birth charts a pictorial view of the metaphysical interface or merely the result of a physically expressed view of a predictable future? The kabbalistic answer affirms that physical entities in no way determine or affect the prior metaphysical realm. Rather, it is this unknowable, non-material realm that contains the determining internal cosmic energy force that will ultimately make manifest the particular channels of energy by which the space-time energy field becomes a reality. The planets simply represent the life-giving forces, the internal or external stimulation in any given area of life.

In astronomy–astrology, we are dealing with combinations of complex life forces and expressions that have become manifest in our physical plane. The process may be compared to the seed of the male, which contains the total complex of life forces along with the channels of energy by which these same internal energy forces subsequently become manifest. It is for this reason that the positioning of the complex mechanism of planetary bodies that were present at the time of a person's birth simply act as the physical interface for the metaphysical interface that encompasses the complete printout of prior lifetimes. In short, the stars determine nothing. They do not compel; they merely impel.

The basic destiny pattern is considered fundamentally unalterable. Therefore, when we have a sequence of experiences that the natal chart could predict with almost 100 percent accuracy, we see an individual dealing with his own incarnation, which is why he was born at a particular time in a particular country to be governed by the particular astral influences of that given moment. Consequently, when we read in the *Zohar* that these astral influences dictate to the enormous and profound extent that they do, it is a result of the reincarnation process, which, in effect, is the consequence of prior flaws in a prior lifetime. From an astrological point of view, the exact time and place of birth does, in effect, reveal the individual's primary—and I stress *primary*—life pattern: His potential, power, attachments, and problems. What the chart is revealing is merely an insight into the pattern of prior incarnations.

For all the inviolability of the basic destiny pattern, however, we have a degree of freedom almost without limitation to determine how our *tikkun* process will be created in our present lifetime. Our natal chart reveals the blinders and restrictions that prevent us from feeling free so that we can ultimately make use of the tools available to us by which we can transcend to another level of consciousness. But those blinders and restrictions are of our own manufacture. We built them in prior lifetimes, but because we created them, we can also break them and ascend to a higher level of consciousness.

This higher level of consciousness will come about through a higher form of meditation and by not only having but living an ideal, spiritual way of life. Then, and only then, can we truly be liberated from the pattern of destiny that seems so unalterable and finally come to grips with our problems. And then we can ascend and alter our initial natal chart.

A commitment to self-knowledge and self-improvement is the first requirement of any individual who wishes to take control of his or her life and alter his or her destiny, but once that commitment is made, the results can be immediate and fulfilling. Not only will the individual be happier in his or her quest to elevate his or her soul, but he or she will find that the pursuit of the global will begin to alleviate a great deal of the suffering initially dictated by his or her *tikkun* pattern. Suddenly, he will notice that much of the confusion and discouragement that once seemed so overwhelming is gradually beginning to disappear. This phenomenon is not necessarily the result of altering his or her natal chart, which is the ultimate goal; it will come about simply because his commitment will result in the improvement and quality of his lifestyle, an alteration without which no one can reach the higher level of consciousness necessary to secure a new chart and thus achieve rebirth.

Anyone recognizable today as a truly spiritual person has gone through this process. Because of the universal *tikkun* pattern, it is safe to say that this individual was not born to such elevation. It was only through self-development that he or she ultimately changed the pattern of his or her life and achieved another level of consciousness. Rav Chaim Vital, the exclusive student of Rav Isaac Luria, actually received something in the neighborhood of 100 different souls in the course of his lifetime, each of which represented a different level of consciousness. Such power is available to anyone who diligently seeks it, but, as with all things worth having, it is not free, and guidance toward the goal is often wanting.

Even the best astrologers can err in the effort to accurately chart an individual's course. They may find flaws or discrepancies in the chart's prediction. But they are of little use unless further investigation is made into the lifestyle of the individual seeking advice. More often than not, the individual will provide information that will indicate ascension to another level of consciousness that can completely throw off the predictions of any natal chart. This is a common weakness of the conventional astrologer who neither considers an alteration of the chart possible nor seeks to know the present life of his client.

In the interpretation of any chart, almost any factor can be regarded as an implication of *tikkun*, but it will not appear to the practitioner who fails to consider the point, because search as he may within his conventional framework, he will not detect subtle shifts in the level of consciousness. Such perceptions do not come from a natal chart. They come from the intuition of the individual astrologer who is truly looking for a synthesis between the planets, the chart, and the direct impressions of the living person. The constructive use of astrology necessitates knowledge not only of what astrology can do for us, but of its limitations as well. The individual's level of consciousness cannot be based purely upon either astrological data or the seeker's intelligence and acquired knowledge. It must be based upon the individual's spiritual lifestyle.

Our present lifetime comprises the sum total of all our previous lifetimes, and only through our comprehension of all these previous lifetimes and all previous experiences can we find in our chart a composite of what we have really been. All that we have been, both good and bad, is contained in our present life chart. Once our faults have been identified, either through a competent astrological reading or through rigorous self-examination, we will be able to pinpoint the negative aspects of prior lifetimes and by growing spiritually change the consistent patterns so as to alter astral predictions and change our destiny.

Skeptics who brand astrology as a parlor game or con game have long asked how the position of the planets at the time of a person's birth can possibly have any bearing upon his or her subsequent lives. Indeed, they have not only the right but the responsibility to ask this question. Just as the most important question a kabbalist can ask is "Why?" the most important obligation of a kabbalist is to answer that very same question with regard to planetary influences, which is what we shall attempt to do at this point.

Planetary and astral influences are nothing more than bodies of energy, both negative and positive. A person is born at a particular time so that when his soul enters its corporeal body, it will absorb the combination of energies dictated by the cargo of *tikkun* carried from past lives. As the soul travels through the metaphysical space between the Endless World and our mundane world, it passes through various levels of energies, picking up what is required of both good and bad influences in terms of habits and attitudes carried over from the totality of its previous incarnations.

Thus the planets are symbols of more than merely physical dimensions. Their placement at the moment of a person's birth can be compared to a program entered into a computer, except that this computer is as massive as the billions of stars and planets of which it is constructed. What emerges is the "software" of the individual's present life with the good and the evil, the strengths and the weaknesses of previous lives neatly formatted from the eternal computer's memory bank. The importance of the placement of the planetary and astral bodies for this purpose is no less than the importance of all the binary bits of information necessary to construct the program sought for a terrestrial computer.

The natal chart thus provides us with what amounts to be a movie of our prior incarnations. Every action of sin and sanctification is stamped there at and by the moment of birth. The moment of birth, therefore, is not a random event. Whether it occurs prematurely or extends to the phenomenon of "the 10-month baby," it is specifically designed to ensure that the individual arrives in this life with every bit of the baggage he accumulated in the last one. The soul without baggage would obviously have no reason to return.

When an individual is born on a particular day at a particular time in a particular place, the kabbalistic astrologer is given an easily read blueprint of that person's psyche and with it, knowledge of how the individual may be able to alter the inborn program and create another whereby he may escape the chains of predestination. It is precisely in this area of free will that this book differs from other books on astrology. Many of them contend there is no exercise of free will. But the kabbalist knows that we might or might not shun our responsibilities and therefore we might or might not live up to our true possibilities, thus free will is unlimited.

The natal chart need not be on a collision course with free will. The man who relaxes before reaching the limits of his capacities is an unhappy failure; the one who explores his limits will be a success. But both can exist within the limited framework of this universe. It is precisely in this area that the science of astrology has not met its responsibility, which is to provide a palatable answer to the apparent contradiction between fate and free will.

If the contradiction has never been successfully addressed by conventional astrology, the parallel aspect certainly has. Witness this story from the *Zohar*[34]:

> *Rav Yosi and Rav Chiya were traveling together and*
> *they saw in front of them two other men going*

along. They saw a third man come up to them and say, "I beg of you, give me some food, if only a piece of bread, because for two days I have been wandering in this forest without tasting anything. I am lost." One of the two men thereupon took out the food that he had brought with him for the journey through the forest and gave him to eat and drink.

Said his companion to him, "What will you do for food, for I am going to eat my own? As you know, we both have taken sufficient food to last us the several days' journey through the forest and if I were to share my bread and drink with you, then both of us will perish." Whereupon his friend replied, "Do I want to eat yours?" The poor man ate up all that he received except a small morsel of bread and the individual in turn gave him even this last piece of bread for the road. Whereupon Rav Yosi felt that possibly they should share with this individual who had completely given of his to this poor man, upon which Rav Chiya remarked, "God does not desire that we interfere at this point with his tikkun process." And then Rav Chiya added, "Perhaps that man was doomed to some punishment and God sent this man to him so as to deliver him."

The two resumed their journey with Rav Chiya and Rav Yosi following at a distance so as not to be noticed. And shortly thereafter, the man who had given his food away became faint. His companion said to him, "Did I not tell you not to give your bread away?" Rav

Chiya then said to Rav Chiya, "We have bread. Let's give him some." To which Rav Yosi replied, "Do you want to undo the merit of this good deed? Let us watch closely, for surely the pallor of death is on this man's face and God prepared some merit for him in order to deliver him."

Meanwhile, the man fell asleep under a tree and his companion left him to carry on as he had told him before. Then Rav Yosi and Rav Chiya saw a fiery adder by him. "Alas for that man," said Rav Chiya. "Surely he will now be killed." Rav Yosi replied, "He deserves that a miracle should be done on his behalf."

At that point, a snake came down from the tree with intent to kill the man, but the adder attacked and killed it, then turned its head and departed. Said Rav Yosi, "Did I not tell you that God desired to perform a miracle for him and that you should not exhaust his merit? For what had been forecast in the stars, was that this man was doomed to some form of punishment, his merit stood up for him."

The man then woke up and began to go. Rav Chiya and Rav Yosi came up to him and gave him food. When he had eaten, they then told him of the miracle that God had performed for him. Rav Yosi then quoted the verse: "Trust in the Lord and do good. Dwell in the land and follow after faithfulness." (Psalms 37:3)

The *Zohar* then goes on to explain:

> *Happy is the man who does good with what he has because he arouses good for the entire universe with righteousness. Because righteousness is the Tree of Life and it arouses itself against the Tree of Death and takes those who are attached to it and delivers them from death. As it is written: "Charity delivers one from death."* (Proverbs 10:20) *And what roused it to do so, you must say is the charity that man does. As it were, he performs it Above also.*

What emerges yet again from this beautiful parable from the *Zohar* is the fact that while the stars impel, they do not compel. The natal chart of the man in question, because of prior incarnations, led him into the wilderness with the opportunity to change his destiny. There is no question that an astrologer reading his chart would have come up with the prediction of his death. A good astrologer, however, knows there is certain information he must not share. He must never predict anyone's death, no matter how evident it may appear in the natal chart, lest he create a self-fulfilling prophecy negating that possible altered state of consciousness that would have changed the grim destiny.

The man in the forest had seized the opportunity offered in a single moment to reach another level of consciousness. He offered to sacrifice his own life for the benefit of another. His companion held that action to be foolhardy. But the *Zohar* demonstrates that the life of this man was forfeit: He was definitely going to die. It was assured, until at the given moment of opportunity, he exercised his free will to obey the precept, "Love your neighbor," (*Leviticus* 19:18) and at that moment, his fate was altered in a fashion the best of astrologers never could have foretold.

Another illustration that the stars impel but do not compel is classically illustrated by the most illustrious sage of all time, Rav Akiva ben Yosef, in the story we already told of the young woman who was destined to die on her wedding day but managed to avert her fate.

For all the sages' use and study of astrology, however, their writings are also filled with warnings against its use in predicting future events. What concerned the rabbis of that time was the aspect of idol worship and the acceptance of a predicted fate that would have negated the individual's free will. Few people today are likely to make false gods of astrological entities, but the danger of fatalism remains. A good astrologer must understand that the natal chart alone does not tell the full story. While the individual is born into certain circumstances over which he has absolutely no say— his parents, his ancestors, his social standing, or for that matter, his physical or mental characteristics—he can, as we have discussed at length, take control of his life and change his natal chart. It must be noted at this point, however, that parents do have a choice in determining the characteristics of their own children, but certain conditions are present at birth as are the tools with which each of us works out our lives. Many astrologers, taking matters no further than this, err on the side of fatalism.

If astrology draws its share of skeptics, then reincarnation, which kabbalistic astrology is based on, attracts even more. Yet the Bible and the *Zohar* are full of references that clearly support the premise:

> *Then the word of the Lord came to me saying, "Before I formed you in the belly, I knew you, and before you emerged forth out of the womb, I sanctified you, and I ordained you a prophet unto the nations. (Jeremiah 1:4-5)*

This verse suggests the idea of repeated existences upon Earth and additionally sets forth the prediction concerning the future of the life of Jeremiah; that he would indeed become a prophet. Does the passage not indicate fate and predictable destiny as opposed to free will? Here, too, the concept of parallel levels provides the reader with deeper insight into the dialogue between God and Jeremiah. This revolutionary idea is further strengthened by the following passage in the *Zohar*[35]:

> *Rav Aba began a discourse on the verse: Counsel in the heart of a man is like deep water, but a man of understanding will draw it out.* (Proverbs 20:5) *"The first clause of this verse,"* he said, *"may be applied to the Lord [the internal cosmic energy force] Who with deep counsel [the wide array of the complexities of prior incarnations] molded events by the hand of Joseph so as to execute His decree, but a man of understanding will draw it out [make manifest the other, altered states of consciousness]."*

This "man of understanding" is exemplified by Joseph who revealed those deeper, more subtle levels that God decreed in this world, whereas "counsel in the heart of man is like deep water" is exemplified by Judah at the time when he approached Joseph on behalf of Benjamin, as explained in my book *The Kabbalah Connection*. What emerges from the *Zohar* are the partial levels that accompany man in his universal travel through time. Joseph represents a level of altered states of consciousness that links up with the outer-space connection—the intelligence level of *Yesod*. Joseph is an individual and a man of understanding "who will draw it out." Judah, linked with the intelligence level of *Malchut*, is represented by the section of the verse that says "Counsel in the heart of a man is like deep water," which is just another way of saying that one who has great knowledge is of no use to anyone if he cannot impart it. It is toward the cosmic level of Joseph, the more subtle reality of consciousness that one draws to, where this new dimension of altered states can be reached. This is the central theme of kabbalistic cosmic consciousness and pure awareness.

Information provides knowledge only if connection is made. The library is full of information, but it remains useless to a person who cannot read and therefore cannot make it manifest. Some people, on the other hand, are "book smart." They know all the facts and figures by rote, but they cannot apply them. We must achieve an altered state of consciousness and pure awareness to make a connection. Joseph knew how. Judah did not.

All of the foregoing may seem complex and abstruse at first glance, but in reality, wholeness and simplicity lie at the soul of the *Zohar*[36], a fact made clear by the following passage:

> *Rav Aba was one day sitting at a gate of Lydda when he saw a man come and seat himself on a ledge overhanging the ground. Being weary from traveling, the man fell asleep. Rav Aba suddenly saw a serpent glide up towards the man, but before it reached him, a small serpent [known in Aramaic as Kustifa Dikuradonna] attacked the serpent and killed it. The man then woke up and catching sight of the [dead] serpent in front of him, stood up and walked away from the ledge. And no sooner had he done so than the ledge gave way and crashed into the hollow beneath it.*
>
> *Rav Aba then approached the man and said, "Tell me, what have you done that God should have performed two miracles for you?" To which the man replied, "Never did anyone do an injury to me, but that I made peace with him and forgave him. Moreover, if I could not make peace with him, I did not retire to rest before I forgave him, together with all those who vexed me. Nor was I at any time concerned about evil that the man did to me. Nay, moreover from that day onward, I exerted myself to show kindness to such a man."*

At this point, one might wonder why the serpent is a recurring theme throughout the Bible and the *Zohar*. Its imagery is essential because it represents the negative side of man. The Hindu aspect, in which the coiled serpent is the sexual power of *kundalini*, is regarded as a positive force, but in the Bible, it is always negative. Sex can be both negative and positive, such as when the desire to have a child alters the state of consciousness making it positive. However, from the kabbalistic point of view, serpent power in and of itself is always negative power, brought on by man's negative activity. When a thief steals, he creates a serpent that will strike him when he least expects it, proving, in short, that crime does not pay.

The point of the preceding parable from the *Zohar*, however, is to show that transformation of an individual to higher spiritual ideals is possible and that consequently, interpretations of a natal chart may be completely outmoded. Obviously, when one takes this more comprehensive approach, which is based on the recognition of a reality much higher than that perceived by our physical senses, it becomes evident that the most important indications in a natal chart will not come from the outer world, but from within. The more we are consciously in touch with our inner self, the more astrology has to offer us. This is not to imply that we now have a new way of manipulating our fate, but rather that astrology becomes a means of clarifying for us the various stages of self-development through which we ultimately can transform our selves and thus produce a new natal chart and a new stage of personal existence.

To further demonstrate how we can literally alter our chart and make manifest our entire life's destiny, I return once again to the *Zohar*[37]:

Such is one as Rav Shimon bar Yochai in whose days the world never required a sign of the rainbow. For whatever punishment was decreed against the world, he could annul it.

One day, he was sitting at the gate of Lydda when he lifted up his eyes and saw the light of the sun darkened three times and black and yellow spots appearing in the sun.

He said to his son Rav Elazar, "Follow me, my son, and let us see what happens, for of a surety, some punishment is decreed above and the Lord desires to let me know."

Such a decree is kept in suspense for thirty days, and the Lord does not carry it out before making it known to the righteous. As it is written: "For the Lord will do nothing but that He reveal His secrets to His servants the prophets." (Amos 3:7)

They came into a vineyard where they saw a serpent advancing like a curl of fire along the ground. Rav Shimon shook his garments and brought his hand down on the head of the serpent, which then came to a halt, though its tongue was still moving. He said to it, "Serpent, Serpent. Go and tell that Supernal

Serpent that Rav Shimon is still alive." It then put its head into a hole in the ground. He said, "I ordain that just as this serpent has returned to its hole in the ground, so will the supernal one return to the hollow of the greater beast."

Rav Shimon then began to pray, and as they were praying, they heard a voice say, "You ministers of evil, return to your place. You band of ruffians, abide not in the world, for Rav Shimon bar Yochai annuls your power. Happy are you, Rav Shimon, that your master is solicitous for your honor at all times above that of all other men."

By this time, he saw that the sun was shining again, and the blackness had passed. He said, "Surely the world is safe again." He then went into his house and expounded the verse: "For the Lord is righteous. He loves righteousness and the upright shall behold His face." (Psalms 11:8)

The black and yellow spots seen by Rav Shimon bar Yochai would be known today as sunspots—titanic storms on the surface of the sun. But in ancient times, their symbolism was one of some great darkness about to befall the world. From the foregoing, we can see that one can often change not only his own personal life destiny but the destiny of the world as well, no matter what the astrological charts might proclaim. Rav Shimon was able to face deadly peril from the serpent and bend it to his will, but the *Zohar* shows that such capability lies within reach of anyone who truly strives for an elevated level of consciousness. With such power, not only are we capable of controlling our own destiny, but we can have a tangible, measurable impact upon the affairs of others as well.

It is absolutely vital that the astrologer inject the essence of these two important passages from the *Zohar* into any aspect of fate prediction versus freewill. Unhappily, most astrologers have no access to this knowledge, and many of them virtually become what the sages feared they might become: idol worshippers giving homage to the signs of the celestial bodies because they know that these bodies do indeed contain the cosmic energies that influence the universe. Knowing this alone, however, they are in no position to do anything that could avert impending disaster. Therefore, they worship, hoping that by such worship, they can quell the wrath of these so-called gods and bring peace on Earth and strength and energy to the universe. Given the wisdom of the *Zohar*, Rav Shimon bar Yochai was truly able to take direct action and by harnessing the power of the Creator, turn a preordained catastrophe aside.

Keep in mind that there is nothing metaphysical or mystical about the idea of prediction. The concept, unfortunately, is so shrouded in the mumbo-jumbo of mysticism that we lose sight of the fact that predictions and prophecies, whether they turn out to be right or wrong, are very much a mundane function of our day-to-day lives. Television commentators, using exit polls, surveys, and computer extrapolations, forecast every presidential election, often with amazing accuracy, even before the polls have closed in

California. Every evening newscast features a weatherman who, by using satellite photos and interpreting isobars, highs, and lows, predicts the weather for the next seven days. Such activities obviously fall under the purview of prophecy, though no one would call it that. There is nothing metaphysical about an exit poll. There is nothing mystical about a weather satellite.

Physicians also are prophets in their own right. They analyze, diagnose, and confidently predict the course of any given illness. Their prognoses are based upon education, experience, and logic. We certainly would not call a physician a mystic, though there is a certain grim parallel between public reaction to the prophet of the Bible and the physician of today. If the prophet of old turned out to be wrong, he was stoned to death. If the physician is wrong, he is sued for malpractice.

So forecasting the future is commonplace to us even as we move into the 21st century. Why, then, is the proposition of forecasting the future through informed study of the stars and planets and their interaction with other celestial bodies a suspect activity? Celestial bodies are harbingers of things to come simply because they make manifest, at given times, cosmic energies applying to individuals born under their unique specific influences. Astrology, the weather, politics—all are merely manifestations of the flow of cosmic energy, and just as we can predict events by means of data programmed into a computer, we can accomplish the same thing, right down to the parameters of the individual soul, by means of the cosmic computer. Through astrology, the cosmic computer is capable of delivering a better, more intimate picture of the individual than that of which he himself is aware.

If we can evolve such skills, then an opportunity is presented that should be sought, learned, and used at will. In relationships, we are frequently fooled by the appearance of what people seem to be, simply because all of us put up defenses against the world in which we live. The drawback to such a necessary survival mechanism is that if we, through our various shields and personas, can fool others, then quite naturally, we also can fool ourselves. Given the truth from an astrological standpoint, we can readily know both the positive and the negative aspects of an individual as well as of ourselves, and if we can do that, our own lives can become a bit easier.

As we have learned through Kabbalah, the roots of human conduct are always mystical. They are concealed from the naked eye, and there is no way of proving anything in the nature of the spirit of man. The soul, however, as an internal force, makes manifest the inner nature of man, so by examination of the soul, we can detect the true motives and aims of those with whom we must deal in this life. Without this capability of inward probing provided by astrology and Kabbalah, all we can do is observe physical manifestations, and those will seldom give answers beyond what the individual manifesting them desires to make public. Through Kabbalah, we can probe the internal mechanism that makes this complicated machine called "Man" really work.

I'm not saying that astrology and a natal chart comprise the answer, but astrology, along with Kabbalah, can provide the fundamental tools needed for the examination of everything around us. This is why I believe that astrology as a study of reincarnation is one of the most important techniques by which the individual can follow his own inner spirit, which is usually concealed even from himself.

Much is made today of solar energy, which is seen as the only alternative to a dwindling supply of natural resources on Earth, but modern scientific knowledge of the sun has little edge on what the *Zohar* already has told us. We are aware of periodic explosive solar flares and sunspots, but so was the *Zohar*. What else was Rav Shimon bar Yochai describing in the *Zohar* story quoted earlier? Now, however, scientists have discovered another solar phenomenon called "coronal holes." These are rips in the sun's surface, which is a blanket of searing gas called the corona. This blinding shroud usually is in character, but occasionally it fails to maintain its uniform equilibrium and a coronal hole develops, through which awesome gusts of solar wind in the form of charged particles come roaring out to disrupt the Earth's magnetic field some 93 million miles away.

This solar phenomenon still is under study, but if astrology is added to the science of astronomy, one begins to understand what the *Zohar* means when it says that there is not a single blade of grass that is not influenced in its daily growth by such vast cosmic energy fields. The astronomer also will realize that the activities of man cause this phenomenon. Astronomy alone will not explain the full extent of the bombardment from the cosmos constantly undergone by our massive planet's atmosphere, but the *Zohar* stretches the dimensions, illustrating that what is happening on a physical level, ineffectual as it may seem to the man in the street, is occurring with equal force on the metaphysical level, affecting the entire universe through channels transferred to us by planetary and stellar entities. To scorn such knowledge simply because scientists are uncomfortable with any entity that cannot be put in a test tube for double-blind laboratory testing is more than unconscionable. In our increasingly complex world, it is dangerous.

*"CERTAINTY IN SCIENCE IS GOOD,
ALTHOUGH IMPOSSIBLE...
CERTAINTY IN RELIGION IS BAD,
ALTHOUGH COMMON."*

—Phil Donahue, *The Human Animal*

CHAPTER SEVEN

PATHWAY TO THE STARS

Aristotle, long ranked as one of the wisest of the Greeks, contemplated the universe and proclaimed that the Earth was its center, with the sun, moon, and stars in majestic orbit around it. At the physical level, as we now know, Aristotle the scientist was wrong. After first reviling him, however, the Christian church finally decided that he was right and made his paradigm such a rigidly enforced point of religious dogma that centuries had to pass before other scientists, such as Galileo and Copernicus, dared set the record straight.

A strange paradox arises from this scenario. Both Aristotle, who could not be certain because he lacked essential data, and religion, which was certain because religion requires no data, were right, not wrong, but neither of them had the remotest clue as to why.

As Abraham knew, and as the *Zohar* has proclaimed, at the metaphysical not the physical level, the Earth is the center of the universe. That is why, search as we will with increasingly vast arrays of radio telescopes, we will never find physical intelligences in other solar systems or other galaxies. Noncorporeal intelligences, on the other hand, proliferate there, and some of them dwarf our feeble intellect.

There was nothing wrong with Aristotle's methodology. He reasoned that the function of inanimate matter must inevitably revolve around the Earth because the Earth was the only plane on which he could physically observe intelligence. Since this observation appeared to be supported by the external appearance that celestial bodies do move about the Earth, his conclusion was impeccably logical. From the beginning, however, Abraham possessed the knowledge extant in the *Book of Formation*, and this knowledge directed him to the internal, metaphysical cosmic energy field, rather than to its external counterpart. He was certain, just not as a scientist or as a religionist, neither of whom to this day have come to grips with the fact that every action of mankind has an equal but opposite reaction in the cosmos, which indeed makes the Earth and its remarkable inhabitants the true center of the universe, regardless of what revolves around what.

There are several spiritual paths by which the metaphysical may be explored. They involve varying levels of consciousness, and they connect with cosmic energy fields that can increase our awareness and elevate our enlightenment. The instrument the *Sefer Yetzirah* and the

Zohar use for this journey is the Bible, which from the kabbalistic point of view is the one spiritual path by which achievement of pure awareness and cosmic consciousness may be achieved. The Bible, therefore, is not merely the document of a religion but the instrument, the medium, by which we can achieve our objective of connecting with cosmic energy fields.

The *Zohar*[38] cites the verse: "And Abraham took another wife and her name was Keturah ... and Abraham gave all that he had unto Isaac, but unto the sons of the concubines [meaning the children of Keturah], Abraham gave gifts and sent them away from Isaac, his son, while he yet lived, eastward into the east country." (*Genesis* 25:1) The *Zohar* then asks how Abraham could have had anything to give to the sons of the concubine after giving all that he had to Isaac, going on to also raise the question of why the verse stresses where Abraham sent the sons of the concubine: ... eastward into an eastern country. The *Zohar* explains that the gifts under consideration were spiritual paths, the highest of which was transmitted to Isaac and the lowest of which were given to his half-brothers, who were then sent "eastward into the east country" where they founded the impure practice of magic and witchcraft. Isaac alone possessed the complete metaphysical system that elevated him to his rightful grade.

It is written *1 Kings* 4:30: "And Solomon's wisdom excelled the wisdom of all the children of the east." Says the *Zohar*, "Herein, is an allusion to the descendants of the very children of Abraham's concubine, who, as is already said, inhabit the mountains of the east where they instruct the sons of men in the arts of magic and divination. It was this very land of the east from which came Laban and Beor and his son Balaam who are all magicians."

The spiritual path open to Isaac was, of course, the Three-Column System described in detail in my book *Kabbalah for the Layman* and reflected by the Shield of David. The incomplete system borne eastward by the sons of the concubines was a Two-Column System and to this day, eastern metaphysical systems are based on duality: Yin and Yang, Left and Right. To brand these Eastern dualistic systems "lower" is more than just an ego trip from those who possess the Three-Column System. The two forms of systems are as different as Newtonian classical physics and Einsteinian physics. Newton's laws remain valid, but Einstein elevated science to a broader, more encompassing level. Newton discussed mass, but lacking knowledge of the atom, his discussion dealt with the external. Einstein, with what could be called a "complete" scientific system, took physics inside the atom itself, and it is no surprise to the kabbalist that the atom, consisting of the triad of protons, neutrons, and electrons, reflects the Three-Column System of Abraham. As Einstein was to do many millennia later, Abraham, in his *Book of Formation*, dealt with the internal aspects of cosmology, whereas Eastern systems, which ranged from China to Egypt, dealt with the externals of astral influences and celestial bodies.

Thus it is easy to see how so wise a man as Aristotle could conclude that the Earth was the center of the universe. Just as Newtonian classical physics had its day, so has the aspect of Eastern astrology. The *Sefer Yetzirah* does not have to wait until tomorrow. It has been with us for a very long time, but to an individual like Aristotle, that sort of knowledge was concealed, just as Einsteinian physics was concealed from Newton. It is within the spiritual path—the aspect of the internal that Abraham shared with Isaac, not his other sons—where the heavy action really takes place even to this day.

Unfortunately, the current scientific establishment is becoming increasingly fossilized by its own particular growing world view. One cannot continue to create formulas and inject the increasing aspect of uncertainty at the same time. This begins to limit our growth and create a specialization that threatens our sense of wholeness. The purpose of our being has also been severely fragmented by individual egos, which have come to make the scientific empire into an individual power base created by the owners of scientific knowledge they themselves have created. When the majority of the people are placed beyond the grasp of true knowledge, then we are truly awaiting the Messianic or Aquarian Age in which knowledge shall be the domain of all, not a select few. Kabbalah itself has been a jealously guarded secret but the time has come for it to reach the masses with its simplicity because in the final analysis, knowledge that is simple is true knowledge. As stated in *Jeremiah* 31:33: "And they shall teach no more every man his neighbor, and every man his brother, saying, 'Know the Lord.' Rather everyone shall know Me, from the smallest to the highest."

The purpose, therefore, of the *Zohar's* explanation of the gifts of Abraham is not to engender a prejudicial attitude toward other paths in the field of astrology and astronomy, but rather to indicate that at this point in history, things have changed. Knowledge is no longer the same knowledge originally received by Abraham, and it is fortunate for us that a fresh approach to science in general and to the fields of astronomy and astrology in particular can now take place. This book is for people who no longer wish to tolerate a state of ambiguity; it is for those who truly understand that change is necessary and are not afraid of handling simple, if not yet accepted ideas. These ideas will provide more answers than conventional information can ever bring.

For those who feel comfortable with Eastern spiritual teachings and who have found the paths of such teachings adequate for what they seek in life, more power to them. But from a *Zoharic* viewpoint, the purpose of King Solomon's declaration was to provide information about a system that will stimulate the thinking process and implant new ideas in the minds, not only of the scientist but of the layman as well. We now must begin to review our universe and build a new concept of it that deals with a holistic picture, rather than continuing to rely on something that encompasses only the fragmented view of a particular scientist who deals with the universe exclusively on the physical, observable plane.

Our technological performance over the past 20 years is really, in effect, the evolution of intelligence itself. When we speak of "knowing" as in the biblical phrase "Adam knew Eve," (*Genesis* 4:1) we speak of connection. This is intelligence at that subtle stage known as cosmic consciousness. It reaches into the subatomic levels of energy, yet the average human cannot grasp more than five to eight percent of his inherent intellectual capacity and the average scientist does little to overcome that limitation. Instead, he has relegated man to a position inferior to that modern golem, the computer. We have come to believe that machine intelligence can solve most of our problems, and that with the computer we are augmenting our own intelligence. As we continue to advance the state-of-the-art in construction of computers, this sense of amplification will increase. One can predict with accuracy that the ultimate demise of all sciences will result in total acquiescence to the computer, at which time it finally will suffer ultimate breakdown. In the long run, however, the golem, a folk lore creature made of mud and animated by magic but devoid of intelligence, will not be able to handle anything that man cannot handle.

Hopefully in the near future, we will come to understand that each subatomic particle in the universe is as intelligent as a human being because the internal activity of a particle is nothing more than an intelligence that directs the movement of that particle. These tiny intelligences eventually evolved into stars, planets, animals, and people. Therefore, at that original atomic level, everyone knew everything and everything knew everyone.

Scientists insist that the evolutionary process follows very strict rules and operates in a highly structured manner and that therefore we will eventually come face-to-face with an alien life form very similar to ourselves. From the kabbalistic point of view, this will never happen because the Earth and her chief occupant, man, are in the cosmos. Stars and other planets evolved from the seven unique energy-intelligences (*Sefirot*), each of which operates within its own frame of reference. Consequently, none are alike, even at the atomic level of intelligence, and there can be no creatures like us, any more than members of the animal kingdom can be like *Homo sapiens*. Cats will never speak or dogs run for office because while cats, dogs, and people occupy the same physical space, they operate on metaphysical levels that are light years apart.

For those who believe that the evolutionary process that governs this planet governs all, and therefore will produce the same sort of creatures, including humankind, in other solar systems, we shall in the next chapter develop the theory of different intelligences and of the particular intelligence of Earth itself. We will show that *Homo sapiens* did not simply evolve, but rather that our species exists because it is the exact composite of particular astral influences.

*"I KNOW NOT WHETHER LAWS BE RIGHT OR
WHETHER LAWS BE WRONG; ALL THAT WE KNOW
WHO LIE IN GAOL IS THAT THE WALL IS STRONG;
AND THAT EACH DAY IS LIKE A YEAR,
A YEAR WHOSE DAYS ARE LONG."*

—Oscar Wilde, *The Ballad of Reading Gaol*

CHAPTER EIGHT

THE CALENDAR

T he Calendar is everywhere. It hangs in the kitchen, sits
on the office desk, nestles with myriad appointments
in the businessman's breast pocket, and rides in
blinking digital numbers on the face of the modern watch.
Without it, we would be lost in the trackless stream of linear
time, condemned like a man in a jail cell to a perception in
which days, months, and years all become one—
monotonous, undifferentiated, and unending. We live
robotically by the calendar, and we take it so much for
granted that we haven't a clue as to its real significance.

The average person is aware, if he bothers to think of it, only
that the calendar is structured around the orbital flights of
the Earth and moon and by measuring them, divides time
into usable fragments. If the celestial bodies provided
nothing more than a time table, however, the internal secrets
of our celestial bodies would remain unrevealed. So

profound is the effect of the calendar upon our lives that no fewer than three such time-measuring systems have been devised, and these individual systems separate the cultures that use them as distinctly as they separate days, weeks, and months. Therefore, it is essential in any study of astrology and astronomy to understand how each system is structured.

The most widely used system, in the Western world at least, is the solar calendar, which defines a year as the time taken by the Earth to complete one orbit around the sun: 365 days, 5 hours, 48 minutes, and 46 seconds. The solar calendar originated with Julius Caesar in 46 B.C.E., but it was based on a solar year of 365 days and 6 hours. To take care of the discrepancy between the 5 hours, 48 minutes, and 46 seconds and the 6 hours, one day was added every four years (creating a leap year). However, even with this adjustment, the calendar lost 11 minutes and 14 seconds each year when compared with the actual solar year. By the year 1582, the Julian calendar (as it was called) was approximately 11 days behind the solar year. On October 4, 1582, Pope Gregory XIII adjusted the Julian calendar to actual solar time by proclaiming the following day to be October 15th and declared that century-years (years ending in a double zero) should not be leap years unless the century year was divisible by 400. This formula provided for an accuracy of within 26 seconds of the solar year on a long-range basis, and the Gregorian calendar became the Western solar-calendar standard.

The second system is based on the revolution of the moon around the Earth. The time interval from one new moon to the next (called "lunation") is 29 days, 12 hours, 44 minutes, and 2.8 seconds. A 12-month calendar—with each month having a value of 29.5 days—results in a year consisting of 354 days, which is 11 days short of the solar year. The Islamic calendar is completely lunar in nature. It is composed of 12 months of 29 or 30 days each.

With the solar calendar, the position of the sun in conjunction with the seasons is always the same. If we use the lunar system, depending on the year, any given month may fall during any of the solar seasons. In the course of just a few years, the cumulative difference becomes considerable, causing the beginning of each lunar year to wander through different seasons of the solar system. Herein lies the problem: In each lunar-calendar year, the end of the 12 lunar months precedes the end of the solar year by approximately 11 days. This means that in 20 years, a holiday that occurs on the last day of the first lunar year will occur 209 days before the end of the 20th solar year, or about seven months before December 31st.

The third calendar is a combination lunar/solar system, which is the system that the kabbalistic calendar follows. This calendar is based upon neither the lunar nor the solar year exclusively but reconciles the two into a mode of calculation in which months are reckoned according to the moon while years are calculated according to the Sun. Since all kabbalistic holidays and festivals occur on days mandated by the Bible according to the lunar month, the lunar year must be reconciled with the solar system to prevent holidays from wandering through the solar period. Thus, *Pesach* always will occur during the spring and *Rosh Hashanah* in late summer or early autumn. This differs from the Islamic lunar calendar where festivals drift through different seasons. Under the lunar system, if we were to start with the lunar month of Aries that corresponds to the solar month of Aries, the following year would see the lunar month of Aries beginning 11 days earlier, eventually drifting through fall, then back through summer.

The reconciliation of the lunar months with the seasons of the solar year is accomplished by intercalation. By adding an extra month, known as an "intercalary month," seven times in every 19 years, the lunar months are adjusted to the seasons of the solar year. Consequently, the 14th day of the Hebrew month of *Nissan,* or *Pesach,* which personifies the cosmic energy force of Aries, never will occur prior to the sun sign of Aries, which runs from March 20 through April 23, the terminating date of Aries. This remarkable mathematical calculation of intercalation provided by kabbalistic scholars demonstrates the enormous importance that our solar system, along with its astral influences, reflects in the lives of all intelligences in this universe.

It might well be asked why go to the trouble of intercalation when it might be simpler to merely adopt the Gregorian calendar with its precisely fixed days and let it go at that. To do so, however, would be to abandon a very specific mechanism within the lunar-solar calendar, a mechanism that the Gregorian calendar does not have. Again, it is important to remember that the calendar is more than merely a timetable for the schedules of man. Indeed, taken on the broad scale presented by the kabbalistic calendar, contemplating the universe as a structure beyond the limitations of physical science does not seem so strange, nor does the concept of using a mathematical formula to describe cosmic influences or, for that matter, recognizing marriage as an electrical circuit.

As stated previously, the kabbalistic calendar adopted a 19-year cycle, with seven of these 19 years (the leap years) having 13 months each. The sum of the months contained in these seven 13-month years comes to 91 months. The figure 91, and the total number of intervening days between each season (which also add up to 91), has profound implications from a kabbalistic point of view. Translated into Hebrew, the number "91" emerges as *Amen* (*Alef,* Mem, *Nun*) the word that many faiths use to end a prayer. The word is a plea for atonement, or, as hyphenated here for the sake of understanding, "at-one-ment." In short, it asks for the blessing of connection, which is what Kabbalah is all about.

The movement of celestial bodies does not, however, cause the resulting number to be 91. Rather, the significance of 91 is as a coded mathematical formula that expresses a specific internal cosmic energy force with a potential astral influence upon our universe.

The physical orbital interplay between the sun, moon, and Earth is the result of a higher cosmic intelligence that is the motivation of physically expressed orbital interrelationships. From a subatomic point of view, all physically expressed orbital entities—including our bodies—are merely the evolvements of prior metaphysically motivated intelligences. If serious moral and ethical changes are to be forthcoming, they must begin with a dramatic change in our view of our environment. The human physical reality does not become motivated without a prior motivating thought. We must condition ourselves to viewing the entire universe within the same frame of reference. Physical expression cannot influence the prior cause of the expression any more than the physical body of man can influence the original DNA.

To find what brought about the need to reconcile the lunar calendar with the seasons of the solar calendar, let us return to the original precept: "Observe the month of *Aviv* [*Nissan*], and keep Pesach unto the Lord your God; for in this month of *Aviv*, the Lord thy God brought thee forth out of Egypt by night." (*Deuteronomy* 16:1)

Why the month of *Aviv*? *Aviv* is the season of spring, when green things begin to bud or break out of winter's bondage. *Aviv* is the season of freedom. It is not by accident that the slang term for aiding and abetting a jail break is to "spring" the prisoner. Spring is Aries, and Aries is the first month of the kabbalistic calendar; only in the month of *Aviv* could freedom begin for the Israelites.

Precepts or mandates of the Bible, from a kabbalistic point of view, are not treated within the framework of religion or tradition. Rather, they are considered in terms of their cosmic significance and importance. The biblical requirement that the lunar system coincide and become reconciled with the seasons of the solar year must therefore be understood within a cosmic frame of reference.

What seems to emerge from this particular section of the Bible is that if the lunar months—carrying with them particular holidays, including *Pesach*—were permitted to go retrograde through the seasons, then the cosmic conjunction event of the lunar-solar, might never have happened. This fascinating panorama of cosmic interplay provided the setting for the Great *Exodus*, which occurred amid an awful upheaval that ultimately terminated an incredible and awesome period of Egyptian history and power. This meant that the Israelite could now tap into the cosmic energy field produced as a result of this cosmic conjunction and destroy the negative cosmic energy force that had enslaved the known world.

The biblical description of the scope of this catastrophe, including the ten plagues, in the *Book of Exodus*, which embodied the forces of the cosmic drama, was not intended to merely record so startling and revolutionary a story, but to demonstrate the kind of cosmic energy that is made available for us to tap into and capture for our own benefit.

During the period of the *Exodus*, a pessimistic outlook about the future was prevalent throughout the world because of the complete estrangement, or negation, of freedom in the form of the internal aspect of the all-inclusive positive energy source. When we are connected to this positive cosmic energy force, we are not slaves to the Desire to Receive for the Self Alone; rather, we can encompass the entire universe, feeling togetherness with everything in it, including our fellow man. The Desire to Receive for the Self Alone is the energy of technology, and since that is what slavery is all about, the same mood prevails today as that which brooded over the Great *Exodus*.

The followers of Moses had been slaves to material energy, but it had the same base—the Desire to Receive for the Self Alone. But the time eventually arrived when the world would be freed through the destruction of this empirical force at its metaphysical level during the Middle Kingdom of Egypt. Today, we see the same slavery to technological energy in that we have become completely bound up with computers. We have become so programmed that we can't think independently and our creative abilities are paralyzed.

Happily, we enter the mood of *Exodus* in the Age of Aquarius. We are ready for freedom, but that freedom can come about only when we can once again get in to tap the original power source: The internal aspect of cosmic energy. That is why the kabbalistic calendar is so important.

The Bible refers to the month of Aries as the *rosh*, or head: "And this month shall be unto you the *rosh* of the months." (*Exodus* 12:2) Rosh also means "beginning," and though "head" and "beginning" are not synonymous, for our purposes they are indicative here of the same thing. At a physical, mundane level, no individual can make manifest any action until he has thought about what he is going to do. After the thinking process has been completed, it is then executed and put into motion.

This is the purpose of the *rosh*, the head—that action taken in this particular month will make manifest all subsequent manifestations on a cosmic level for the next 11 months. This is the secret that was revealed through the *Zohar*. Aries is the head, the beginning.

In Abraham's time, the day of this massive practical application of tapping into the cosmic power source lay far in the future. The concepts it contained, although already mentioned in the *Sefer Yetzirah*, were for Abraham. He could make use of them, but Moses would have to wait until the time of the *Exodus*.

Why was the precept of Sanctifying the New Moon mentioned just prior to the tenth plague, which was the plague of the slaying of the first-born? It is because the first-born possess *rosh*-energy, a concept more fully explained in my book *The Kabbalah Connection*, and for the Israelite, it was imperative to destroy the head of Egyptian power and force so that it could never again revert to the energy force that enslaved Israel.

Today, we find ourselves again dominated by this same energy force, although it is not equal to nor should it be compared to the energy force that the Egyptians displayed and controlled at the time of the *Exodus*. Today, this force is called "high tech." The Egyptians had their Valley of the Kings, with its marvels of pyramids, embalming, and magic. We have Silicon Valley, where microchips are made to function as only the human mind functioned before.

To ensure a complete safe and free future, a complete removal of the dominance of energy matter, which pertains the Desire to Receive for Itself Alone, is necessary. We must return to the ultimate computer—the human brain. Anything else is surrender. To physically escape that which dominates the world landscape is, of course, impossible. The highest mountains of Tibet and the wildest deserts of Outer Mongolia have been invaded at this point by the microchip in one incarnation or another. But if we yield to the negative aspects of high tech, we will eventually have to pay the price of the golem.

This point was explored some 30 years ago, by author Whitley Strieber in his terrifying futuristic novel titled *Warday*, first published in 1984. The story recounts what passes for life in a balkanized United States following a limited nuclear war not vast enough to trigger nuclear winter and annihilate all life, but enough to destroy both the United States and the Soviet Union and to make them poor vassals of the surviving super-powers of Britain and Japan. In *Warday*, it is neither the destruction of a few cities nor the famine and plague that follow that destroys the United States; it is the high-voltage electromagnetic pulse from a couple of 50-megaton bombs detonated well above the Earth's atmosphere, set to destroy in the blink of an eye every computer system upon which the fabric of our lives depends.

Thus, in *Warday*, the microchip-created golem to which we had surrendered everything—all records, all history, all the mechanics of production and social interaction—fell and we fell with it. Strieber may prove to be a modern prophet.

The scientific basis for all of the advanced technology we know today has brought with it problems that many people feel are probably insoluble. Under the impact of computer technology, we ultimately run the risk of becoming so inundated with information that our very survival may be in jeopardy. Computer technology has certainly brought us a great deal of benefit, but so ubiquitous have computers become that any serious breakdown could cripple an entire country. At the time of *Exodus*, a specific date in the month of Aries, a confrontation occurred between two internal energy forces, which were not represented by physical matter but which were so potent that when the event occurred, through kabbalistic knowledge of cosmology, it destroyed the head (the *rosh*) of the material energy that existed as Desire to Receive for the Self Alone. A similar confrontation, with a level of equal impact on future generations, is pending, and it will give those of us who can learn to wield its power the ability to remain free.

This early version of Star Wars took place in the days of Moses, and the Israelites were given information that ultimately allowed them to be the victors. They would be able to win by tapping into the all-inclusive positive energy to subjugate the negative energy that had kept them in bondage. We know, as described in my book *Kabbalah for the Layman*, that this all-inclusive positive energy came first, and when it is tapped, darkness is banished and our enemies, who roll throughout the negative energy of the Desire to Receive for Oneself Alone, are overthrown. Such bondage was not exclusive to Moses' day. It still reigns, if not always so brutally in our time, but as always, once the all-inclusive positive energy is established, it automatically does away with the negative force that is the root of all evil in the universe.

Enter a darkened room and light a match, and you've done away with darkness. It is that simple. The two do not appear together. Light is not merely the absence of darkness, nor is darkness simply the absence of light. Darkness is a very potent cosmic energy force as the *Zohar*[39] makes clear: "In the beginning, in the Ein Sof, there was no coloring of any kind whatsoever. Neither white, neither black, neither green, neither red. No coloring whatsoever." We learn from the *Zohar* that each color represents an internal energy force, and this includes black. Consequently, when the cosmic energy of the all-inclusive energy is prevalent, it removes the internal energy force of positive darkness, which was the internal energy force of the Egyptians.

The biblical battle between the forces of Light and darkness, when the Israelites were given the three-column system, is revealed in *Exodus* 12:7: "And they shall take of the blood and put it on the two side posts and the lintel upon the houses wherein they shall eat," and it is emphasized here because it has bearing on events that were to come millennia after the *Exodus*.

As the sun was going down, the Israelites in Egypt slaughtered the lamb, the blood of which was designed to turn aside the Angel of Death, indicating that the transfer of cosmic energy-intelligence that produces the metaphysical DNA for the negative, destructive energy flow takes place at this particular time. The story of the *Exodus* lies now in the mists of history, but the time correlation for this negative energy remains the same today as it was then.

For Abraham, the *Exodus*, and modern man, timing was and is of the essence—whether modern man consciously knows it or not. If one changes metaphysical DNA that which already has been designated by the DNA is also changed. One may thus alter the course and consequences of a year or even of a lifetime. The timing of an event is equally important when knowledge of the information process being transferred or transmitted at a particular time is available. Therefore, the essential timing of *Exodus*, as stated in the *Zohar*[40], was on the 10th and 14th days of *Nissan*.

The negative cosmic energy field and negative cosmic terminals are functional at the setting of the sun. Consequently, when Abraham received information concerning the exiles and saw that the Israelite of the future would have to suffer, he was receiving a metaphysical DNA prediction. This does not mean, however, that such predictions cannot be altered. They can, but only if the Israelite subsequently makes use of the information at hand. His own particular cosmic energy field contains a composite of the Three-Column System in which his Desire to Receive for Himself Alone is harnessed and placed into a triad. When the triad position of the circular concept effectively has been reached, then an altered state of consciousness is achieved. This new frame of reference provides a changed, higher, parallel level of existence where a completely new set of rules and principles now govern. A new program, to speak in the vernacular of the computer, has been loaded into the corporeal mainframe of the individual. A computer carries a program that can be updated from time-to-time without altering the physical state of the computer, and the same holds true with a human. While his body does not seem to have undergone change, a new metaphysical DNA, with all its subsequent ramifications, can become manifest. This is the parallel level of existence; parallel because some original aspects and cosmic energy—the physical structure, for example—remain the same.

The Israelite at the time of the Great *Exodus* made the outer-space connection. In so doing, he left behind his entire prior existence along with its programmed metaphysical DNA. He no longer retained the state of cosmic energy that was dominated by the priesthood of Egypt. The program had been changed because the Israelite had learned how to connect with and tap into the cosmic energy from the all-inclusive positive energy by transforming his very essence and being. The Israelites had thus taken a leap forward to another state of cosmic consciousness, leaving behind the level of consciousness of a multi-incarnated soul.

The fall of Adam predetermined the metaphysical DNA of intelligence, creating the cosmic soul presence of the Deluge, the Tower of Babel, the generations of the Great *Exodus*, and the repeated appearance of souls reincarnated for those very events. For the very first time, the altering of a metaphysical DNA had been accomplished by a nation as a whole. In the past, this almost impossible feat had been reserved for the select few. With the *Exodus*, however, a celestial cosmic event of vast magnitude was established within the cosmos, never again to be lost but to remain eternally for future generations to tap into. Even now, it provides an opportunity to change the predetermined and predestined metaphysical DNA to which the particular cosmic intelligence of the reincarnated soul had previously been programmed. No longer would humanity be compelled to live by the agonies of predetermined programming triggered by the incarnated cosmic soul. Through knowledge, plus the determination to upgrade one's cosmic spiritual level to an altered state of consciousness, this change of DNA was now possible. It should, however, be made crystal clear that if a decision to upgrade one's level of spirituality or spiritual growth has not been formulated, then knowledge and connection cannot and will not serve as a substitute for internal spiritual progress.

Over the centuries, the Israelites learned this and wept. This race, which by the hand of the Almighty had once had the power not only to bring mighty Egypt to its knees but to eventually march through the Promised Land virtually immune to the warlike resistance of its inhabitants, was to endure subsequent centuries of diaspora, persecution, suffering, and ultimately the nightmare of the Holocaust. All of these events occurred simply because they let slip their level of spirituality and hence their command of the Three-Column System given to them under Moses. Their slide began with the creation of the golden calf and a rebellion against God that kept them wandering in the wilderness for 40 years before they were permitted to enter the Promised

Land. But the power they once held still exists, and it still can be tapped into "between the evenings": "And you shall keep it up until the fourteenth day of the same month: and the whole assembly of the congregation of Israel shall kill it in the evening." (*Exodus* 12:6)

But what does "between the evenings" mean? The *Zohar*[41] provides us with a clue:

> ... that is the time when judgment predominates Above and Below... also it was at this time [between the evenings] that Israel's exiles were foretold to Abraham, as it is written: "And when the sun was going down, a deep sleep fell upon Abraham, and lo, a horror of great darkness fell upon him." (Genesis 15:12) "Horror" signifies one Supernal "crown," which represents Egypt; "darkness" is a second such, representing Babylon; and "great" refers to the Edomite (Roman) exile, which was to be the hardest of all. Thus it is seen that the Israelites did not go out of Egypt until all the Supernal powers and principalities that were Israel's enemies had been brought to naught. But when these things had come to pass, the people were free from their domination and brought under the Holy and Heavenly sway of the Holy One, blessed be He, and were joined to Him and to Him alone, as it is written: "For unto Me, the children of Israel are servants; they are servants whom I brought forth out of the land of Egypt." (Leviticus 25:55)

Thus, the final curtain on the great Middle Kingdom of Egypt came down. Far out in interstellar space, celestial harmony seems to be the order of the day. During the day, we can see no planets or stars at all since the sun is so much brighter to our eyes than they are. We can study the celestial Heavens only in the evening, and it is only then that we can observe the beauty, the loneliness, the power, and the unspoken word that each celestial body seems to offer.

It is difficult to know the truth about the origin of our planetary systems. Indeed, understanding the beginning and evolvement of our celestial system suffers from an overdose of scientific prescription called speculation. Since we were not present when it all began, how can we legitimately come to any conclusions as to how and why it came about? Astronomers once thought all planets moved around the Earth in complicated orbits. This belief persisted until 1543 when the Polish astronomer Nicolaus Copernicus created his epoch-making breakthrough, showing that the planets, the Earth included, revolved around the sun. Acceptance of this new way of thinking, however, did not really change people or the way they were to think about themselves in relation to the vast cosmic structure suddenly revealed.

The three types of calendar systems formulated by civilizations to measure the passage of time are highly sophisticated vehicles of great accuracy, pinpointing the solstices, which give us our seasons, and other pertinent data concerning the day and night cycles, which dominate the most important aspects of all of Earth's realities. Our planet rotates from west to east. The sun still is seen rising in the east and setting in the west. Little in common daily reflection has changed since the Copernican revolution. We take its function for granted; hang the calendar on the wall, and forget it. That, perhaps, is why even when we summarize all the data and evidence concerning the three basic calendar systems, we find that we still have not come to grips with Kabbalah's most important question: Why?

Is it merely by chance that the Western world accepted the Gregorian calendar, based on the solar system, while the kabbalists established one with a lunar-solar base, and the Moslems opted for only a lunar measurement? Is there more to these events than meets the eye? Could there have been, and possibly still be, mitigating cosmic circumstances that mandated this three-calendar matrix? Now that we have accustomed ourselves to questioning the obvious, removing the framework in which most of us have been cloaked through our educational system, we shall make an attempt to investigate the motivating factors.

First, let us probe the unseen metaphysical cosmic energy forces upon which these calendar systems are based and ask what cosmic intelligence dictated the West's acceptance of the Gregorian calendar.

The lunar month, which had served as the basis for many early calendars was superseded in Roman times by Julius Caesar who created the Julian calendar in 46 B.C.E. This calendar was based on a solar year of 365 days, 6 hours. As noted previously, this is about 11.5 minutes longer than the solar year. The Julian calendar was finally corrected in the year 1582 by Pope Gregory XIII, whose version became known as the Gregorian calendar. Although the Gregorian system has a discrepancy of 26 seconds from the actual solar year, it is estimated that it will take 3323 years to build up to a single day.

The Chinese calendar, which dates back to 2397 B.C.E. is divided into 12 lunar months of 29 or 30 days each and is adjusted to the solar year by the addition of extra months at regular intervals. The years are arranged in major cycles of 60 years.

The Islamic calendar, which reckons time from July 16, 622 C.E., is entirely lunar in nature, so the year consists of 354 days. Thus, their festivals wander through the solar seasons. Certainly, a need must have been felt to stabilize this measurement of time and to fix the days in orderly cycles dictated by the celestial bodies, but it has never been done. Is there, then, a metaphysical intelligence that has programmed the Moslem world not to adopt the more logical systems of the Gregorian and kabbalistic calendars? Can we assume that some internal energy field central to the Moslem people directed their choice of a lunar system?

The lunar-solar calendar reckons time from the year of Creation, 3761 B.C.E., a time frame generally accepted by fundamentalist Christians. Such a date, set for the creation of all things, does, of course, collide head-on with anthropological findings indicating that mankind, in a more primitive mode perhaps, may have occupied the Earth for as long as one million years, while fully developed Cro-

Magnon men walked the landscapes of Europe 10,000 to 15,000 years ago. It is a collision, however, that will not bother the kabbalist, who is accustomed to dealing in different frames of reference and varying levels of consciousness. Suffice it to say that fixing the date of Genesis by counting the ages given in the Bible for the patriarchs at their respective deaths is sufficient to create a working calendar, whatever the system of its basis.

Neither celestial charts, sundials, nor astronomical values established in different parts of the world, which are essentially unchanged to the present time, can provide logical reasons for the Jews, Chinese, Moslems, or Western world to have chosen their particular calendar. While stability of the calendar can to a large degree be attributed to the celestial order of our universe, reasons for the choices made remain a mystery.

On July 20, 1969, the Apollo 11 astronauts became the first humans to set foot on the moon. From that moment on, the moon became one of the best-known celestial bodies outside of Earth. When Neil Armstrong and Edwin Aldrin Jr. returned home after making the first human footprints on the moon, they brought back scores of photographs as well as rock and soil samples. Scientists could now speculate about Earth-moon history as never before, although they could study the moon's mineral content, but little else. The moon, Earth's constant companion, unlocked some of the great mysteries of our universe, but it failed to answer the question of why the Earth has a constant companion in the first place. It is precisely this lack of understanding of the internal cosmic forces that exist within these two celestial entities that prevents a further in-depth probe of the moon.

Nothing of real scientific value for humans seems to have emerged from this very expensive exploration of our constant companion. Unfortunately, science persists in its backward method of investigation, beginning its probe from a superficial physical level, then proceeding inward to the more subtle layers and dimensions. Continuing our own investigation into the internal, cosmic intelligence of the moon and following the principles of kabbalistic interpenetration, we return again to exploring the calendar systems adopted by the three regions of our world: The solar calendar used by the West; the lunar calendar used by the East, or Moslem world; and the lunar-solar calendar used by Israel, in the center.

An examination of the ultimate physical manifestation seen on a mundane level and of the astral influences in effect at that time can tell us many interesting things about ourselves, about nations, and even about parts of the universe. In providing us with an in-depth penetration of astral influences and reconciling them with the internal aspects and characteristics of people, nations, and universes, the *Zohar* immediately provides us with this sort of information rather than requiring us to grope for it from a physical level as does the scientific community. The kabbalistic world view provides us with the root manifestations, thereby avoiding a great deal of the research and development that must go into these areas when we deal with matters on a physical plane, inasmuch as physicality has an infinite number of layers that literally conceal that which is below. No matter how much technology and research can do in analyzing the seed of any particular plant or vegetable, they still will not penetrate much further than the superficial layers of these particular entities.

It is through a profound study of the *Zohar*, which is based on the Bible and its narrations, that we gain this kind of internal subatomic perception that otherwise would be eternally blocked for us. What we are dealing with when discussing the "why" of the particular segments of this universe and its population of intelligences or the "why" of choosing particular calendar systems, is a very valid question from a kabbalistic world view.

Let us answer this question first by exploring those cosmic intelligences that mandated the acceptance of the solar or Gregorian calendar by the Western world.

Historically, the Western world is represented by Rome, which gave it the bulk of its laws, its political methodology, its culture, and even the root of its many languages. The *Zohar*[42] considers Rome the Left Column of the *klipot*, which is the aspect of world physicality, the aspect of negativity, the aspect of the electron. That Rome (and its nation descendants) would be ruled by an expansion of the metaphysical aspects of the Left Column is demonstrated by technological advances that represent a refinement of the Desire to Receive for Oneself Alone.

The Gregorian calendar was accepted by the Western world because the west is ruled by the sun—the primary aspect of negativity, fire, and the intense Desire to Receive.[43] Wherever there is an intense Desire to Receive, technological advancement will be manifest. When we speak of high tech, better systems, more sophisticated hardware, we are in effect discussing the channels for the transfer of energy, not the energy itself. These channels are the vessels that create physical expressions of energy. As noted before, that which we are transferring, the internal element, whether it be a television show, radio programming or the activation of a satellite in space—in short, anything and everything that begins and becomes actualized in one place and appears elsewhere—has, at the moment of becoming actualized, already appeared metaphysically elsewhere and everywhere. For example, the pressing of a button at any space center to activate a satellite is the secondary, or physical, expression of a thought process that cannot be revealed until it becomes clothed within a physical vessel. In this case, the pressing of a button has become the very vessel that reveals the thought of the individual who decided to press the button. The physical transfer of the thought, which is the energy of internal intelligence, then appears to take place. The fact is that this internal intelligence has already activated the instrument in space by metaphysical means. The action that will take place in space remains in a passive, potential state, awaiting the activation of the physical vessel by means of the pressed button to reveal the thought process.

This revolutionary outlook is comprehensible now by virtue of quantum mechanics, which describes the universe as one interrelated whole. The deeper the scientist probes the universe, the more new sophisticated detection devices will be developed. In the foreseeable future, we will be able to detect the thought process as an intelligent energy force transcending the limitations of space and time. The thought, which is a non-material energy force, will pervade the entire universe simultaneously, faster than the speed of light. Western high tech is headed toward instantaneous, faster-than-light vessels, or channels, that will immediately reveal intelligent energy forces at the metaphysical level. This leaves us with an exciting note that belongs, for the moment at least, in the realm of science fiction: Instantaneous transfer of matter, such as a populated starship teleporting from the vicinity of Earth to Barnard's Star or Alpha Centauri. Scoffers should be reminded that all space travel once lay in the realm of science fiction, including that which took us to the moon in the Apollo program and that which now takes us into orbit aboard the space shuttle as readily as a Greyhound bus takes us to Kansas City. The fact is that if we are on a correct path both physically and metaphysically, there is nothing magnificent at all about such a concept.

Atoms are all around us, but they remain in a passive, potential state until a vessel or channel reveals and makes them manifest. A chair or the wall of a house is no more than a composite of atoms that becomes manifest by the physical vessel known as wood or stone. From a kabbalistic point of view, atoms are forms of intelligence: The electron as the Desire to Receive, the proton as the Desire to Share, and the neutron as the Desire to Receive for the Sake of Sharing (Desire to Restrict). Thus, atoms contain all the interrelated aspects that act as metaphysical conveyances of our thought processes. Stretching this concept one step further, when a person wishes to throw a stone at a window, the glass has already received this information by means of the activating thought process that transcends space and time. In effect, the internal process of shattering began long before the actual physical act of impact takes place. If the stone ultimately does not reach the glass, the internal, metaphysical process of shattering will not begin or take place either.

The research and development of highly sophisticated systems for the transfer of energy, which is nothing more than intelligence, thus lies within the domain of the west.

It does not, nor will it ever lie within the grasp of the east where the lunar calendar prevails, with one exception: Japan is part of the east, yet the Japanese have proven their ability to develop highly sophisticated systems based on the technological Desire to Receive. This is explainable by Japan's own historical self-definition as "the land of the rising sun" or *Nippon*, which means "land of the origin of the sun." For all of its geographical and cultural links with the east, Japan has been metaphysically aligned with the west for centuries.

The Desire to Receive indicates motivation—a drive that depends upon intensity. The greater the intensity of the desire, the greater the ambition and, as a byproduct, the possibility of more intense selfishness and greater power for evil. Rome displayed these negative characteristics as did no nation before it. Romans of the totally materialistic imperial period boasted that "all roads lead to Rome," and in a fine display of the Desire to Receive for the Self Alone, indeed they did. It therefore is no wonder that Rome and the western world that followed it adopted the Gregorian calendar, based upon the sun and the negative Left Column of the Three-Column System.

Nor is it any wonder that the east, dominated by the Moslem world, adopted the pure lunar calendar. The *Zohar*[44] spells it out: "The children of Ishmael will at the same time rouse all the people of the world to come up to war against Jerusalem ... for I will gather all nations to war against Jerusalem to battle...." (*Zechariah* 14:2) Ishmael is the Right Column of the *klipot*[45]—the aspect of positivity, the aspect of the proton, which rarely, if ever, is in action. The lunar system, which is the aspect of water and Cancer, is the Right Column ruled by the Crab, which in turn is ruled by the moon. This Right Column is typified by static immobility. It indicates a Desire to Receive for the Sake of Sharing, and this virtue has always been characteristic of the Arab. Even today, his hospitality, his warmth to strangers, his love of sharing is legendary. He is of the Right Column, and his society will unlikely embrace high technology. From the beginning, cosmic intelligence mandated that he would follow a lunar calendar with no regard to shifting days and seasons.

This leaves only the Central Column of the Three-Column System, and there, in a manifestation of the Desire to Restrict, lives Israel. Of Israel, the *Zohar*[46] says:

"And all the children of Israel will assemble in their various places until the completion of the century. The Vav will then join the Hei and 'they shall bring all your brethren out of all the nations for an offering unto the Lord.' (Isaiah 66:20)"

Only through the Central Column can there be an ultimate joining of the Left and the Right for a positive expression of the all-embracing unification. Only the Israelite, who all too often through history has forgotten the system given to his forefathers at the time of the *Exodus* but who will ultimately remember it, can bring about such unification. Did the Israelite for this reason choose the lunar-solar calendar? Or did the lunar-solar calendar choose him? The answer is obvious.

The calendar system, then, was neither an accident of Creation nor the product of whimsy—and neither is an individual's life. Our lives do not consist of a series of coincidences and chance encounters. When we study kabbalistic astrology, we not only have to learn about the physical nature of the universe, but we must also make contact with its metaphysical aspects. The two aspects, astronomy and astrology, must work together if a more comprehensive world view of the universe is to be achieved. Kabbalah provides the underlying universal laws and patterns, which science ultimately defines in its own way as manifestations of the physical universe. We should, however, always bear in mind that the physical universe is not the only plane of consciousness and intelligence. The levels of energy upon which the process of creation is always at work are infinite.

Unfortunately, these infinite metaphysical levels go undetected by modern instruments of the physical sciences. This book in particular and Kabbalah in general seek in some way to prepare the individual for, and lead him into, an expansion of consciousness. The first step toward this goal is to understand that what we are referring to are not concepts beyond the reach and realm of science. Let us not forget that microbes and single-celled animals were in an invisible world until the invention of the microscope and that some of our solar system's planets remained in an unknown world until the invention of the telescope. X-rays and cosmic rays were the stuff of science fiction and fantasy until we developed instruments to measure them and make them manifest.

As science evolves and more things become visible, we should not forget that the scientist somehow never seems to be overly concerned about *how* things come into being. This, I believe, is the vital role that Kabbalah plays in providing a total picture of the scheme of things. Then, through the physical sciences, we can proceed to understand the processes by which these initial rules of intelligence and evolution became manifest.

The principles of Kabbalah, being spiritual, must of necessity transcend the notions of independent, private prejudices or delusions of racial superiority. Ultimately, the student of Kabbalah will have the opportunity to rise above these beliefs instilled in him from childhood and become uplifted by a spiritual light—the Light of Wisdom.

Mankind always has been divided into various ethnic groups, and each race has developed according to its own kind of civilization. Through the evolutionary process on a physical, mundane level, man reveals a diversity that continues today, with some nations rising and some nations falling. But it is the internal aspect that governs the ultimate variations and self-expressions. Man can be united if there is an understanding that at the root level, man is unified, if not exactly created equal. We are not created equal, but that does not mean that one individual is more important than another. The more expansive our cosmic consciousness becomes, the more we will recognize the harmony and direct relationship between ourselves and the process of evolution of the universe as a whole. Then man can come to live with his fellow man, provided each individual understands the all-embracing unity of harmony that exists in a diversity where each person is independent of yet interdependent with the other. Now we come to a revealing passage in the *Zohar*[47] that concerns itself with the days of the Aquarius-Messianic period:

> *In the year seventy-three [of the sixth millennium], all the kings of the world will assemble in the great city of Rome. And the Lord shall cause celestial collisions and will shower on them fire and hail and meteor stones until they are all destroyed, with the exception of those who will not yet have arrived there.*

Here is a Divinely orchestrated catastrophe showing the interrelationship of man and the universe. Is it prophecy? Possibly. Could it find grim application to the United States in years to come? One thing alone is certain. The aspect of sharing, which this country has displayed, as has no other nation in history, from the great waves of immigration through the rebuilding of Japan and Germany after World War II, is what has made a superpower of the United States. If ever we lose that aspect of sharing, we can expect to fall as surely as Rome and Egypt did.

Several instances related in scripture commemorate great cosmic phenomena, where the actions of forces of the universe are directly related to the termination of kingdoms. Another example:

> Rav Yitzchak once drew close to the foot of a mountain and there saw a man sleeping under a tree. Rav Yitzchak sat down. Suddenly and without warning, the Earth began to quake violently and became full of fissures. The tree was uprooted and fell to the ground, and the man beneath it woke and cried with a loud voice, "The quaking of the Earth signals a warning to you that a new ruler is being appointed in Heaven who will cause great misfortune to Israel."

This cosmic catastrophe described in the *Zohar*[48] passage above is similar to the one mentioned in *Joshua* 10:11:

> The Earth underwent a bombardment of hail and stones. As they fled from before Israel, and they were going down to Beth-Horon, the Lord cast down great stones from Heaven upon them and they died. There

were more dead from hailstones than they who died by the sword of Israel.

The meteor stones fell in such great numbers that more people died in the torrent than were slain by the forces of Israel. Did such a cataclysm happen to mark the end of some point in history? In truth, just such a phenomenon had previously taken place during the Great *Exodus* to bring about the end of a great kingdom, the Middle Kingdom of Egypt:

> *There fell an awesome hail, such as had not been in Egypt since its beginning.* (Exodus 9:18) ... *These stones fell mingled with fire.* (Exodus 9:23)

The *Talmud* states that the stones that fell on Egypt were hot, (*Babylonian Talmud, Tractate Berakhot,* pg. 54b) fitting to the description mentioned in the *Zohar*. Later, the story of the revolt of Korach and his party contains another reference to cosmic upheaval:

> *And the earth opened her mouth and swallowed them up. All Israel that were around them fled at their cry, and there came out a fire from the Lord and consumed the two hundred and fifty men that offered incense.* (*Numbers* 16:32)

Similar descriptions come from various places mentioned in the *Books of the Prophets* in which the destiny and fortunes of nations relate to great catastrophes. Isaiah received the awesome mission of prophesying the destruction of the

Babylonian empire and spoke in terms of awful cosmic movements in the cosmos:

> *For the stars of Heaven and their constellations shall not give their light.... Therefore I shall shake the Heavens, and the Earth shall remove out of her place in the wrath of the Lord and in the day of His fierce anger.* (*Isaiah* 13:10-13)

It does appear that with the fall of the Babylonian kingdom, a cosmic event or change took place within the celestial nature of the stars in Heaven, the light of the moon and sun was dimmed, and, more startling, that the earth moved away from its center. Isaiah spoke in a similar manner when portraying the loss of the land of Israel to Sennacherib:

> *The foundations of the Earth do shake... the Earth is utterly broken down, the Earth is clean dissolved, the Earth is moved exceedingly.... The Earth shall reel to and fro like a drunkard.* (*Isaiah* 24:18-20)

What seems to emerge from these passages is that they contain an account of the interrelationship between what befalls the Heavens or the altering of the given order of our universe, such as the Earth's rotation and the rise and fall of kingdoms, or in a more subtle frame of reference, the rise and fall of the individual. What I have endeavored to show in citing such passages is that cosmic upheaval and cosmic determination and influences have some connection with the actions of man.

Was Joshua's miracle in stopping the sun then a natural phenomenon or does man actually have the ability to move and motivate stars, repel their negative influences, and tap into their positive energy forces?

The scriptural descriptions of cosmic catastrophe indicate a need for a new approach to celestial mechanics. What has become apparent is that the determining factor of cosmic upheaval is directly linked to the actions of man. This revolutionary viewpoint makes it possible to understand the evolutionary process of the transition from world religions based on planet worship to the cosmic and monotheistic religion of Judaism, with its concept of the all-inclusive positive energy force that is the Desire to Share—in short, the Creator.

This is how and why the Israelites, starting with the patriarch Abraham, were able to cast off their early belief in the deity of the stars, a belief shared with other nations, and embrace the one, all-inclusive God. Abraham received the knowledge of astral influences in its entirety, with the conclusion that it was to the internal positive energy force that we were to connect and tap, and not the external intelligence of the negative energy force. As stated in the *Zohar*,[49] when a nation has succumbed and worships the aspect of negative intelligence, then we can expect cosmic upheaval, which is the result of that nation's connection to and worship of the negative energy forces.

But we also need to remember that the worship can assume many forms—even the worship of technology.

"AND HE SAID IN THE SIGHT OF ISRAEL,
'SUN, STAND STILL UPON GIBEON, AND MOON,
STAY IN THE VALLEY OF AJALON.' AND THE SUN
STAYED UNTIL THE PEOPLE HAD AVENGED
THEMSELVES UPON THEIR ENEMIES."

—*Joshua* 10:12-14

CHAPTER NINE

THE COSMIC CALENDAR: PREDESTINATION?

P robably the most bizarre and incredible story of cosmic miracles is the one that marked the career of the successor of Moses, Joshua ben Nun. While pursuing the Amorites at Beth-Horon, Joshua directed the sun and the moon to stand still. And they did so, we are told, for the course of the whole day so that an Israelite victory could be assured: "For the Lord hearkened onto the voice of a man. For the Lord fought for Israel." (*Joshua* 10:14)

Are we then to assume on the basis of the *Book of Joshua* that at some time during the middle of the second millennium B.C.E., the Earth's rotation about the sun was interrupted by the command of a mortal man? Joshua, speaking to God, implored this startling cosmic disruption before the eyes of Israel, and these two celestial bodies, whose cosmic DNA of energy dictates that they move along their precise, predestined orbital paths, obeyed as if this very interruption had been cosmically present in their computerized programming from the time of Creation.[50] And, indeed, it was. Joshua's halting of the sun and the moon was no different than Moses' parting of the Red Sea, as the *Zohar*[51] indicates:

> *Said Rav Yitzchak, "In that hour when the Israelites drew near to the sea, the Lord summoned the great angel appointed over the sea and said, 'When I created the world, I appointed you over the sea, making at the same time a past contract with the waters that they must divide for the Israelites in their time of need. Now their hour of trial is come and they must cross the sea.'" It therefore says: "and the sea returned to its strength." (Exodus 14:27)*

> *"The [Hebrew] word leitano [Lamed, Alef, Yud, Tav, Nun, Vav], his strength, also suggests litna'av [Lamed, Tav, Nun, Alef, Yud, Vav], his compact [that the sea had with God when He created the universe]."*

The natural tendency and internal energy-intelligence of a stream propels it in a constant, uninterrupted flow. The splitting of the Red Sea required the energy-intelligence of the seas to remain in suspended animation for the time that was required for the Israelites to cross. In the same fashion, God, at the time of Joshua's need at Beth-Horon, implemented this startling cosmic disruption of the natural function of the cosmos, which, through metaphysical DNA, dictates that the sun and the moon move along their precise, predestined paths. At the moment when Moses commanded the Red Sea to part, the seas of the entire world obeyed his command, (*Rashi* on *Exodus* 14:21) changing their internal DNA according to the computerized program inserted by God from the time of their creation.

The story of Joshua at Beth-Horon is certainly beyond the belief of even the most pious in today's world. We have all experienced the solar year, consisting of 365 days, during which the moon circles the Earth and the Earth circles the sun. So for the sun and the moon to come to a complete standstill is simply an incomprehensible cosmic event unless we can face the realization that celestial intelligences, otherwise known as celestial internal cosmic energy forces, can be and are directed by man in his altered state of consciousness. If this sort of revolutionary thinking is acceptable, then we can proceed to investigate and to ultimately understand how the Earth was forced out of its regular motion.

The question is how, where, and when did cosmic domination occur that can lead us to believe that Joshua's miracle with the sun and moon was more than a fascinating fable concocted in the mists of time? The key is found in *Exodus* 12:1-2): "This month shall be unto you the beginning of months. It shall be the first month of the year to you." This is the Bible's first mention of the zodiac sign Aries as (*Rosh haChodashim*) the first, or head, of all the months and the head of the zodiac system.

The key words in this *Exodus* verse just quoted are "to you." With that phrase, cosmic control shifted at the time of the

Exodus, leaving the children of Israel—and with them, all mankind—in control. Without that control, the Ten Utterances later handed to Moses on Mount Sinai (including "Do not kill" and "Do not steal") would have been beyond the grasp of a species that always had killed and stolen as naturally as it had breathed. By shifting control to "you," or mankind, the Creator conferred upon His creation an ethic and a responsibility by which mankind would be bound from that day forth.

Now, with their newly granted control of the negative cosmic energy by which men had killed and stolen in an unconcerned manifestation of their Desire to Receive for the Self Alone, they were suddenly able to control and rule themselves. With the fall of Egypt's Middle Kingdom, mankind could tap into the positive energy, and Aries became the first of all the months, thus bringing all celestial bodies under the domination of man. Joshua, knowing this, was literally able to halt the rotation of the Earth for the Israelites in apparent defiance of all natural law.

The month of the *Exodus*, which occurred in *Aviv*, the spring, became the first month of the year. Consequently, a strange celestial event was created dictating that from the moment of the *Exodus* onward new cosmic dimensions and forces came into being. With the end of the Middle Kingdom in Egypt, when the Great *Exodus* took place, a new age of cosmology was ushered in.

Before attempting to decode the significance of Aries as the first sign of the zodiac, let us explore another aspect of this verse. According to Nahmanides in *Parus HaRambam*, (*Exodus* 12:2), this inauguration of *Nissan* (Aries) as the first of the months of the year was the first precept ordained upon Israel as a nation. Are we to presume that this precept—the sanctification of the new moon—was of such importance that there seemed to be an urgency in proclaiming this precept while the Israelites were still in Egypt, rather than merely including it within the framework of the main commandments of the Bible, which were promulgated in the wilderness at Mount Sinai? What is the significance of this precept that was ordained even before the children of Israel witnessed the declaration of "I am the Lord, your God" (*Exodus* 20:2) or the moral and ethical doctrines of "Do not murder" and "Do not steal"? (*Exodus* 20:13) Another point that must be raised in our investigation of this verse is the fact that this abstruse precept preceded the final plague, the slaying of the firstborn. (*Exodus* 12:29) What hidden cosmic secret lies in the precept's position among the plagues?

In this connection, a striking observation should be made as far as conventional astrology is concerned. Conventional astrology clearly began when man began to observe the heavens. He was very excited by the moving bodies of the observable solar system against their starry background. He noted that some of the paths these planets took somehow seemed to be related to his own situation and background.

Thus, from a conventional astrological viewpoint, man developed a systematic pattern of celestial events that appeared to have direct parallels with the affairs of Earth:

the obvious connection between the moon and the tides, red Mars as the bringer of war, beautiful blue Venus as the symbol of love and harmony. All conventional astrology originated when man began to observe the Heavens. Under the system of astrology that originated with Abraham, however, and certainly from the point of view of the new age of physics, what we see in the Heavens with even the most powerful of telescopes might not actually exist. The field of conventional astrology has always been a wasteland, forever at odds with the scientific world, assuming (without ever knowing why) that Aries heads the zodiac and basing all the zodiacal signs upon Greek or Egyptian mythology (neither of which has a place either in kabbalistic or biblical views of the subject).

The zodiac as described in the Bible and the *Sefer Yetzirah*, which preceded the Bible, is certainly at odds with conventional astrology as to when the signs of the zodiac were discovered. We obviously do not agree that they were discovered 2000 years ago, as is generally accepted in scientific circles. Kabbalah contends the zodiac was discovered about 3700 years ago. It had always been there, of course: A thin belt of stars stretching across the sky against which the sun, moon, and planets can be seen to travel. Because all these celestial objects lie near the ecliptic (the plane of the Earth's orbit), the zodiac is quite narrow, extending only nine degrees on either side of the ecliptic. Mathematically, the zodiac is divided into 12 segments, or signs, at 30 degrees of arc. The 12 arcs correspond to the 12 constellations, which are stars that form the actual outlines of the 12 signs.

The fact that the signs are mentioned in the Bible, the *Sefer Yetzirah*, and the *Zohar* is clear evidence of an awareness of kabbalistic astrology. For various reasons, however, this knowledge has been neglected, with the consequence that both astrology and knowledge of the zodiac have been attributed to the Babylonians, the Greeks, and the Egyptians. History has completely omitted any acknowledgement of kabbalistic astrology.

The rhythm of the moon, from a kabbalistic cosmological viewpoint, is of such importance that the coming of every month is specifically celebrated. In this case, the "celebration" is not used in a conventional manner, which implies an observance by rote with little or no knowledge of its reason or origin. Inasmuch as we know that what we are discussing are the cosmological effects of each sign of the zodiac, we will shortly understand that we're dealing with the tapping of cosmic energies, and what has been provided for us through any form of traditional celebration is really a sophisticated procedure—an intricate and precise method by which we can tap into these particular energies for our benefit.

On the Sabbath before each *Rosh Chodesh* (New Moon), the day of *Rosh Chodesh* is heralded with a special, unique service during the Sabbath service, and there are prayers by the congregation asking God to make the new month one of life, blessing, joy, and peace. The mystics and kabbalists of Safed in the 16th century treated the day before *Rosh Chodesh* the same way, fasting and regarding the eve of the new month as a small *Yom Kippur* or Day of Atonement.

Thus, on the day preceding the first day of the lunar month, kabbalists would make a pilgrimage to a particular spiritual teacher. In fact, this is a common modern tradition, the purpose of which is to connect with the new cosmic energy that shortly will appear.

On the day preceding a new month, and also on the 15th day of that month, we at Kabbalah Centre in Israel make pilgrimages or mystical tours to specific righteous people. We ask their extraterrestrial intervention to provide us with the opportunity to tap into the positive cosmic energy that will flow during that particular month and to prevent the negative cosmic energies from flowing under that sign of the zodiac. We ask to be provided with the means of preventing their negative influences from reaching us and becoming manifest in our mundane affairs.

The day of the New Moon itself is considered a minor festival, and again, "festival" is just another definition of a cosmic event for which prayers have been established. Prayers for us are channels by which we can tap the cosmic energy that appears on that particular day. All such holidays and festivals are cosmological time frames for astrological influences that the naked eye certainly cannot observe. Consequently, what has been provided for us in that mass of words called the Bible is merely the timetable of those cosmological events; when they take place and what forces they bring to hand. These events are referred to as festivals, or in the Bible, as precepts by which we can tap into that incredible cosmic energy force for our use and prevent negative astral energies from reaching us. Nearly all who pray in good faith, whether Jew, Moslem, or Christian, will testify that their prayers are frequently answered, but few, if any of them, know why. How much more powerful their prayers would be if they did.

Seven days after *Rosh Chodesh*, the date of the New Moon, there is another "traditional" ceremony for the *Kiddush Levanah* or the sanctification of the New Moon. This actually was the first precept to the Israelites in Egypt, preceding the ten of Judeo-Christian bedrock, and it concerned the initial tapping of the positive cosmic energy that alone could offset the power of the Egyptians who knew how to tap into the moon's negative energy. Moses proclaimed this initial tapping necessary to make manifest the tenth plague of *Exodus*, the Slaying of the Firstborn, for which the Israelites made use of the lamb. In modern parlance, the lamb was the software by which the program of a world totally consumed with negativity could be erased.

The *Exodus* was not for the Israelites only. All who were enslaved became free on that day, and since the lamb was the software of the process, it is easy to see why Aries is the first of months. Yet over thousands of years, no attempt has ever been made by conventional astrology to explain this phenomenon. This remains one of the underlying causes of the dichotomy that exists between the science of astronomy and astrology. Astronomers offer no answers at all. They are content, in their lack of understanding, simply to dispute the validity of astrology, which they write off as a mere myth with no real physical effect. Neither the five senses nor conventional science can grasp the reality of unseen internal forces, and what science cannot put in a test tube or under a microscope, science cannot believe.

To further stress the importance of freeing astrology from its prison of mythology and place it in its proper position in science, we must turn to Rav Isaac Luria in *Lekutai Torah*, who discusses the importance of this precept called the Sanctification of the New Moon, saying, "This precept of the Sanctification of the New Moon would now begin with the month of *Nissan* inasmuch as this month will now be considered the first month." This first month of *Nissan* falls during *Aviv*, or spring.

Another coded message in *Exodus* 13:3-4 substantiates the importance of this particular season:

> *And Moses said unto the people, "Remember this day in which you came out from Egypt, out of the house of bondage, where, by strength of hand, the Lord brought you out from this place. There shall be no leavened bread eaten. This day you go forth in the month of Aviv [Spring].*

These particular biblical verses are contained in our daily prayers, and as Rashi commentating on *Exodus* 13:3 declares, we learn from this particular passage that it is a daily obligation of the Jew to recall the Great *Exodus* in his daily prayers. The word "meditation" might be substituted for "prayer" here, since it is by means of meditation that we make use each day of the cables that free us from linear time and project us into that consciousness in which there is no time, space, or motion. This makes time travel a tool that is most effective on the 15th day of *Nissan*, which is brought about by a conjunction of the solar-lunar months. It is only in the month of *Nissan* that freedom can be proclaimed. Slavery is a condition where one is subjected to the astral, physical, and external energy forces of our planet and of our universe and to man's Desire to Receive for the Self Alone.

This is why *Exodus* stressed that "This day you go forth in the month of *Aviv* [spring]." This is why the Israelites were freed from bondage. The conjunction of the solar aspect of *Nissan*, Aries, and the lunar cycle constituted a team of incredible energy forces working to produce a celestial confrontation at the time of the Great *Exodus*. It was a confrontation during which the Israelites created a cosmic energy force called freedom. Even today, one cannot have freedom this energy force simply by wishing. The contemporary student of Kabbalah has the same power at his or her fingertips, but to grasp it, he or she must apply discipline and meditation. Tradition alone simply will not get the job done. Tradition is little more than an owner's manual spelling out how connections must be made and buttons pushed.

It should be obvious by now that dependence solely upon the solar calendar, as in the case of conventional astrology, or upon the lunar year, as Moslems do in pursuit of the art, effectively short-circuits any application of kabbalistic astrology. Only under the kabbalistic lunar-solar system can the 15th day of *Nissan* coincide with or be in conjunction with the Aries aspect of the solar system. Without this conjunction, we would miss that particular vital combination of celestial forces under which the required variety of cosmic forces pervades the universe. The method of connection was disclosed in the form of the precept of *Kiddush haChodesh* to enable the Israelites, at the point of the *Exodus*, to control their entire destiny and not be governed by the ensuing 11 months of negative astral influence.

This, then, is the importance of that particular "day" mentioned in *Exodus*, and we can understand why its proclamation became the first precept. Knowledge is connection, and as indicated earlier, Genesis spells out the synonymous relationship between knowing and connection: "Adam *knew* Eve, his wife, and she conceived and bore Cain." (*Genesis* 4:1) This "knowing" goes beyond the mere biological coupling by which mammals reproduce their kind. In the case of Adam and Eve, it might be compared to two people who know the same thing about sports, fashion, physics, or the weather. When they know like this, they somehow seem to have a greater affinity with each other. Both are connected to the same thing. Consequently, when we *know* of astrology—when we understand cosmic consciousness and its internal intelligence—it is then alone that we are tuned into the proper channel. That is why kabbalistic astrology goes to such great lengths to provide knowledge of cosmic energy rather than merely knowledge of one's natal chart. We are primarily concerned with knowing, and when we know the internal and external aspects of cosmic energy, we are in a position to connect. When we are in a position to connect, then we have the precept of *Pesach* given at this particular time.

The most distressing aspect of what was occurring in Egypt and throughout the world during the time of the Israelites' bondage was not so much the gravity of all the suffering they had undergone but the dampening of the human spirit—the freedom of thought and action so vital to independent individuals. *Pesach* was able to address that specific problem and provide freedom to the spirit.

We hear so much today about how the problems arising from technological advances are probably unsolvable because they are so numerous and profound. Most people harbor feelings of hopelessness almost unprecedented in human history. With the disturbing technological and environmental crises that seem to crop up almost daily, I am inclined to believe that we will remain on the brink of catastrophe as long as we cannot free ourselves from the problem of not being free, of being computerized and losing all initiative in the process. Small wonder that so many people believe that if present trends continue, our form of technological civilization must inevitably collapse.

Today, as never before, we are ruled by an unprecedented interconnectedness of effects. Something that happens in China directly influences American perceptions and living patterns. Political conflicts in the Middle East seriously affect the world economy. Tyranny in the Sudan reverberates on Wall Street. This growing interrelationship has frustrated the attempts of poorer nations to develop effective industries or to manage their economies, and their frustration has spawned terrorism. With speculation of what still might come—nuclear war, an irretrievably polluted environment, damage to the ozone layer, acid rain—fear, gloom, and hardship prevail, but this whole chorus of woes is nothing more than a replay of history.

It is the Great *Exodus*, on stage for yet another encore, and the metaphysical connections by which the Israelites dealt with the first *exodus* are still in place and functional for all who have the will and the knowledge to use them.

internal

*"SPACE, THE FINAL FRONTIER. THESE ARE THE
VOYAGES OF THE STARSHIP ENTERPRISE,
ITS FIVE-YEAR MISSION: TO EXPLORE STRANGE
NEW WORLDS, TO SEEK OUT NEW LIFE AND NEW
CIVILIZATIONS. TO BOLDLY GO WHERE NO MAN
HAS GONE BEFORE."*

—Star Trek

CHAPTER TEN

BIBLICAL SPACE TRAVEL

For all of its futuristic setting, there is nothing new about *Star Trek*, the now-classic television adventure series in which Captain James T. Kirk and his intrepid crew hurtled at warp nine speed across the cosmos, nurturing good, battling evil, and looking with awe upon life forms and intelligences never dreamed of on Earth. What the Starship *Enterprise* did as fiction for five years, kabbalists have been doing spiritually for centuries, and they needed no technological hardware to accomplish their mission.

The Bible is filled with references to what can only be called space transportation systems. The purpose of this book is not merely to recount these references, but to propose how we can effectively make use of this information now to delve more deeply into the mysteries of our universe and to understand the control such mysteries exercise over our cosmic destiny. This book proposes that those who can ascend to a higher or altered state of consciousness can become welded into the outer space connection and that conventional religion should not picture itself as a static, dogmatic community but rather as a channel by which such higher consciousness can be achieved.

The Bible's recorded events are merely coded presentations of more intelligent and higher forms of extraterrestrial life, which can assist such lower forms as us by causing changes for the better in our metaphysical DNA. Before the Fall, Adam could communicate with extraterrestrial levels of unsurpassed intelligence in cosmic energy fields. Denied that ability by the advent of sin—which is to say, our insatiable Desire to Receive for the Self Alone—we now struggle back toward that lost paradise of Eden, still hungry "to boldly go where no man has gone before." We are in the process of planning and testing space vehicles for interplanetary travel, but the most sanguine of scientists offer little hope that we will ever be able to replicate the Starship Enterprise and extend our physical sphere to the stars. They are so far away that even travelling at warp one speed, the speed of light aboard the *Enterprise,* most of them would not be accessible in a lifetime. They are not, however, inaccessible to the kabbalist, as is evidenced by descriptions of "space vehicles" in the *Zohar* and the Bible. Let us browse among some of the available models.

One of the first accounts of such a vehicle was revealed when Moses and the Israelites were traveling from Egypt to the Promised Land. They were accompanied on their trek across the wilderness by a spaceship that looked like a pillar of cloud: "And the Lord went before them by day in a pillar of cloud to lead them the way, and by night in a pillar of fire." (*Exodus* 13:21) The *Zohar*[52], exploring the implications of this peculiar passage, explains it as follows:

> *Rav Yitzchak said, "The expression 'and the Lord' means the all-inclusive intelligence energy force and His Council. This illustrates what we have been taught," said Rav Yitzchak, "that the patriarchs were the Shechinah's chariot. Abraham is indicated by the words 'walked before them by day' (the aspect of the positive, Right Column magnetic energy force), Isaac by 'in a pillar of cloud' (the aspect of the negative, Left Column magnetic energy force), Jacob by 'to lead them the way' (the aspect of the neutral, Central Column magnetic energy force), and King David by the words, 'by night in a pillar of fire' (the aspect of all three forces unified and now manifested). These four patriarchs together formed the supernal chariot, for the assistance and guardianship of Israel so that she might walk in harmony, completeness, and peace."*

The biblical description of the vehicle is set forth in terms by which space transportation could be understood in those days—as a chariot. That higher forms of life intelligence existed long before the Great *Exodus* is well established in the *Zohar*[53], particularly at the time of the tower of Babel:

> *We read: "Blessed be the name of God from everlasting to everlasting; for wisdom and might are His."* (*Daniel* 2:20) *Whenever God permitted the deep*

mysteries of wisdom to be brought down into the world, mankind was corrupted by them. He gave Supernal Wisdom to Adam, but Adam utilized the wisdom to familiarize himself with the negative grades as well until, in the end, he attached himself to the evil side and the fountains of wisdom were closed to him. After he repented before the Lord, parts of the wisdom again were revealed to him in the book given to him by the Angel Raziel. But through that same knowledge, his descendants again abused it. Adam gave this book of wisdom to Noah, who indeed benefitted mankind with its knowledge, but, like all the rest, he later abused it as well.

Thus we see that by virtue of fragments retained later on, people built a tower of hubris and did various kinds of mischief until their language was confounded and they were scattered over the face of the Earth, bereft of wisdom or purpose.

In the Age of Aquarius, however, the Lord will again cause wisdom to be disseminated throughout the world, and the people will worship Him, as it is written: "And I will set my spirit within you." (*Ezekiel* 36:27) In contrast with generations of old, who used this wisdom for the ruin of their world, the verse continues in reassurance for those to come: "I will cause you to walk in My statutes, and you shall keep My ordinances and do them."

But the vehicles so graphically described in *Exodus* are not the only ones the patriarchs were able to move through the cosmos. Witness this one from *Ezekiel* 1:14: "And the living creatures ran and returned as the appearance of a flash of lightning."

Ezekiel was the outstanding prophet during the exile. He was exceptional and unique among the ancient prophets as the only prophet whose sphere of activity lay outside the Land of Israel. However, this was not the only exceptional characteristic of Ezekiel's prophetic career. He was unique both in the nature of his vision and in his mode of expression.

The most remarkable section of the *Book of Ezekiel* is the opening chapter. Here the prophet describes his personal experience with the Divine Chariot. This gave rise to a system of esoteric thought known in kabbalistic literature as *Ma'aseh Merkavah*, the speculation of the Divine Chariot. This branch of esoteric teaching dealt with the natural sciences and *Merkavah* metaphysics.

In accordance with the teaching of the *Babylonian Talmud, Tractate Hagigah*, pg. 13a, the account of Creation is not to be expounded in the presence of more than one person and the story of *Merkavah* not even to one unless he is wise. However, the less important parts of the *Merkavah* may be taught to those of high moral standard and perfection.

Support for this permission may be found in daily morning prayers in the Liturgy of the Festivals. The famous *Merkavah* hymn, *ha'aderet ve'emunah le'chai olamim*, referred to as "the sons of the angels," is recited by many congregations every Sabbath in the morning prayers and in all temples on the Day of Atonement. Above all, the first chapter of the *Book of Ezekiel* is the selection for the *Haftorah* reading on the first day of *Shavuot*, a fitting theme for the anniversary of the revelation on Mount Sinai.

The significance of the patriarchs as chariots of varied energy-intelligence, has been discussed at length. The *Midrash* in *Genesis Rabbah* 82:6 declares, "The patriarchs are the *Merkavah* (chariot)." Ezekiel's vision suggests that the soul of man—any man—is endowed with the capability of acting as a chariot. Ezekiel's Ofanim Hayot and *Galgallim* (wheels, living creatures, and wheel work) (*Ezekiel* 1:16) form the Divine Chariot in outer space, and the patriarchs were the Divine Chariots on the terrestrial level. Ezekiel's vision brought the Glory of God down to the mundane sphere. The Glory of God, in kabbalistic terminology, is the force or energy source of God, and to bring it down to the terrestrial is to connect with and control the Divine Chariot.

Let us pause for a moment to explore some of the phenomena that we have witnessed in our own time and in our own mode of expression. Practically every scientific invention of the 20th century was predicted in a science fiction story. Who does not remember the formidable Buck Rogers when he first wielded his ray gun in *Armageddon 2419 A.D.* or aliens wreaking destruction on the Earth with an invisible heat ray in H.G. Wells' *War of the Worlds?* It was exciting stuff, and except for the aliens from other planets, much of it either is or soon will be science fact.

Science fiction deals with change. Scientists today realize that science fiction is a window of the future. Human-powered flight-aircraft, once thought of as impossible, are on the drawing boards. When we come to the realization that the mind supersedes and surpasses physical energy, then how far are we from mind-powered aircraft?

This is precisely the vision to which Ezekiel was referring. To the kabbalist, metaphysics is learning the rules of a beautiful game that consists of the natural laws and principles of the universe. These rules, unfortunately, are not well understood, and are in the domain of a select few. Most of the time, science plays the game at a much lower level and confusion reigns. To work at the level of root and origin is very rare.

Many years ago, social worker Betty Hill and her husband claimed to have been abducted by short, bald aliens who took them aboard a UFO where they were subjected to medical examination. The tale catapulted the Hills into the tenuous role of celebrated UFO experts. Large numbers of people believe in the existence of UFOs and believe them to be manned by extraterrestrial visitors. For the present, the existence of UFOs may be science fiction. For the Bible, however, the Age of Aquarius is the dawning of space travel as Ezekiel knew it when he described his spaceship in these words:

> *And their appearance and their work was, as it were,*
> *a wheel within a wheel, and when the living creatures*
> *went, the wheels went hard by them; and when the*

living creatures were lifted up from the bottom, the wheels were lifted up. (Ezekiel 1:16-20)

This is a clear reference to space vehicles and the extraterrestrial aliens that man them. The *Zohar*[54] interprets the vision of Ezekiel in the following manner:

And the living creatures ran and returned as the appearance of a flash of lightning. The concealed lights were revealed, and although revealed, the energy-intelligences of concealment, remained as before. At times, they appear, and at other times, they remain concealed. At times, they appear as one color and then at other times, another color. Sometimes, the energy-intelligence of one of the Names of God is used, and immediately another craft appears with another Name of God. No one can tolerate or remain fast in its presence.

This is the secret meaning of the above-mentioned verse: "as they depart and appear in a flash." So, too, for the observer, they appear, depart, and appear again within one's own intelligence, unlike the prophets who observe the Lower terrestrial level and comprehend the Upper Level connecting with cosmic consciousness of the celestial level, the Angel Met-at-ron. The Angel Met-at-ron rules over and controls a fleet of 4500 squadrons and its 45 million energy-Light intelligences.

Each time the fleet departs or enters, 1500 galaxies
tremble and vibrate. A flaming fire follows Met-at-
ron's departure from and re-entry to her base. Within
this fiery flame are engraved the various letters of the
Shem HaMeforash, the secret of the mystical Names
that control and direct extraterrestrial activity.

Is anybody out there? The *Zohar* seems to think so. Indeed, we are not alone in the universe, though there are no others sharing humankind's corporeal form, nor are there any who are independent of human activity.

It is at once exciting and frightening for a world that only a short while back thought of itself as both the spiritual and physical center of the cosmos. The *Zohar* maintains that humankind controls and diverts extraterrestrial activity, so, still in keeping with the foresight of science fiction, how does one respond to an extraterrestrial alien invasion? Will humankind be at the mercy of the aliens? According to the *Zohar*, spiritually advanced aliens travel in the form of pure intelligent energy that moves faster than the speed of light. Does this necessarily spell the doom of our universe? Are we really helpless in the event of attack where the undamaged victor could dictate terms to a disarmed and helpless loser?

The Earth in upheaval has been recorded in the Song of Deborah in *Judges* 5:4-5, which states: "The Earth trembled and the Heavens dropped ... the mountains melted." King David recorded a similar calamity when he wrote in *Psalms* 68:8: "The Earth shook, the Heavens also dropped at the presence of the intelligence of *Elokim*; even Sinai itself was moved."

What seems to emerge from the preceding verses is that both Deborah and King David appear to have been unaffected by the calamity that they themselves recorded. How?

"Now as I beheld the living creatures, behold, one wheel upon the earth by the living creatures, with his four faces." (*Ezekiel* 1:15) The wheel is actually the consciousness level of *Neshama* (Soul), although the Hebrew word for "wheel" usually indicates the consciousness level of *Nefesh* (Crude Spirit). The reason for this is to reveal the steps in the cosmic connection with extraterrestrial spacecraft. When the Crude Spirit has elevated to the consciousness level of Soul, then the connection has been completed and the "spacecraft" is at hand.[55]

It is an admitted premise that we cannot know the truth about the origin of the planetary systems, which came into being billions of years ago. In fact, the question of the origin and evolution of the solar system suffers from the label "speculation." It is frequently said that most, if not all theories postulated by scientists wind up with a "but we cannot be certain" comment at the end. It is, I believe, only common sense that prompts us to raise the question: If we were not there when it all started, then how can we legitimately arrive at any conclusion as to how it was formed?

The *Zohar*, therefore, provides refreshing relief for those lost in the maze of computer printouts on matters of the cosmos. The *Zohar* describes the primeval chaos and just about everything else there is to know about our universe.

Contacts among celestial bodies are not limited to the celestial bodies themselves. In this book, I have described the cosmic connection between man and the cosmos and have endeavored to show that man determines the activity of our solar system. The reason that cosmic catastrophe occurs so infrequently in historical time is precisely due to human activity, which has undergone very little transformation. Still, change has occurred more than once without conclusive explanation.

Without Kabbalah, the stories of catastrophe as they are reconstructed from the records of man and nature can never be complete. The *Zohar* provides the missing bits of information that we can employ toward a better understanding of the nature of man and his cosmic environment.

The development of the Jewish religion comes under a new light and dimension. The information presented on Mount Sinai was not an attempt to establish religion as a mode of behavior. Rather, its aim was to help humankind trace the origin and evolution of our universe; to understand the relationship between the cosmos and man, and more importantly, man's purpose within the complexity of it all. One may ask why, if there are so many civilizations in the universe, none ever has communicated with us. The *Zohar*[56] answers "Because one must achieve a level of consciousness and awareness for contact with intelligent life in the universe." Earth's radio presence, a mere 50 years old, is not the route to establish contact, and it constitutes, at best, a worthless exercise.

The universe is teeming with life—intelligent-thought life—amid the hundreds of billions of stars that stud the galaxies. Why can we not have Ezekiel's vision to witness it all?

Again, the *Zohar*[57] provides us with the answer:

> *Said Rav Shimon, "Alas for the blindness of the sons of men, all unaware as they are how full the Earth is of strange and invisible beings and hidden dangers. Could they but see, they would marvel how they themselves can exist on earth."*

Our search to determine man's place in the cosmos is only half the task. The other half is to establish the sort of power and influence man has on his environment—terrestrial and extraterrestrial—and to understand the power that nature holds over us. The spaceships of Ezekiel and *Exodus* are at our fingertips if only we can rise to the occasion by elevating our souls to that state of consciousness where these spaceships can be utilized. The Starship *Enterprise*, in all its journeys, never faced so sublime an adventure.

"THE END-ALL OF KNOWLEDGE IS TO KNOW THAT WE CANNOT KNOW EVERYTHING. BUT THERE ARE TWO SORTS OF NOT KNOWING. THE ONE IS WHEN A MAN DOES NOT BEGIN TO EXAMINE AND TRY TO KNOW BECAUSE IT IS IMPOSSIBLE TO KNOW. THE OTHER EXAMINES AND SEEKS UNTIL HE COMES TO KNOW THAT ONE CANNOT KNOW EVERYTHING."

—Baal Shem Tov

CHAPTER ELEVEN

HUMAN STAR WARS

I t is apparent that today, we find ourselves in a state of worldwide crises. For the very first time, we are faced with the awesome reality of the possible extinction of the entire human race and all forms of life on our planet. Nevertheless, the resounding words of the prophet Ezekiel provide some hope for the future and a welcome alternative to the threat of a nuclear catastrophe. But with the new discoveries of the 70s in astronomy, we have been brought face-to-face with a phenomenon more outlandish and more bizarre than any encountered ever before in the history of science: The catastrophic gravitational collapse of stars, which predictably results in a black hole or a naked singularity.

Being an utterly lawless entity, a singularity should cause totally chaotic and random influences. It is to this very chaotic possibility that the prophet addresses himself. The Israelites, through whom the energy-intelligence program system was revealed in coded form on Mount Sinai and then subsequently decoded through the *Sefer Yetzirah* and the *Zohar*, were provided with detailed laws and instruction by the Tetragrammaton through Moses and Rav Shimon bar Yochai. This did not necessitate any clairvoyant powers, but rather, the knowledge that would permit a connection with space vehicle systems channeled by the intelligence-energy. This is what I refer to as the outer-space connection space vehicle to which Adam, before the Fall, had been connected. He ate of (that is, connected to) the Tree of Life and was destined to live forever until he decided to take the lower universal life course of good and evil.

"And the Lord God formed man of the dust of the ground and breathed into his nostrils the breath of life; and man became a living soul." (*Genesis* 2:7) The *Zohar*[58] provides the following interpretation of this verse: "The breath of life was enclosed in the earth, which was made pregnant with it like a female impregnated by the male. So the dust and the breath were joined, and the dust became full of spirits and souls."

God breathed into Adam the breath of life and Adam became a living creature. Here the words "into his nostrils" unveil the mystery of the entire verse and the secret of life itself. The code word "nostrils" reflects the cosmic energy-intelligence of *Zeir Anpin*, the outer-space connection. Life, which is cell division, is caused by *Zeir Anpin* inasmuch as all living entities—human, animal, and plant—are composed of exactly the same physical material before and after death. The difference is that in life, cells divide,

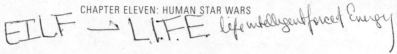

EILF → L.I.F.E. life intelligent forced Energy)

chemical reactions take place, and molecules change, whereas in death, none of this takes place. Such is the energy-intelligence force (life) in the mysterious creation of all things in the universe. The connection is the Tetragrammaton (*Yud, Hei, Vav* and *Hei*) the channels are the laws and principles of the Bible.

"This is the book of the generations of Adam (man). In the day that God created man, in the likeness of God made He him." (*Genesis* 5:1) Following the *Zoharic* tradition of unlocking the mysteries surrounding the tremendous supply of stored intelligence and knowledge contained in the invisible universal brain bank, we find an explanation that decodes this verse.

> *Rav Aba said, "God did indeed send down a book to Adam, from which he became acquainted with the Supernal Wisdom. It came later into the hands of the 'sons of God,' the wise of their generation, and whoever was privileged to pursue it could learn from it supernal wisdom. This book was brought down to Adam by the Master of Mysteries, preceded by three messengers. When Adam was expelled from the Garden of Eden, he tried to keep hold of the book, but it flew out of his hands. He then pleaded with God with tears for its return, and it was given back to him in order that wisdom might not be forgotten of men and that they might strive to obtain knowledge of their Master. Tradition further tells us that Enoch also had a book, which came from the same place as the book of the generations of Adam. When God took him,*

he showed him all Supernal mysteries and the Tree of Life in the midst of the Garden and its leaves and branches, all of which can be found in his book. "[59]

The intelligence, knowledge, energy, and its manifested physical laws of expression always have been in existence just as they are now. Looking backward in time, there was no less total universal intelligence at an earlier time than is now recognized in our day. The cosmic life cycles of our universe, which appear as a continuous, expanding cosmology experience, change in a physical evolutionary process, but the energy- intelligence itself remains above and outside space-time principles.

Where, then, is this book referred to by the prophet Ezekiel that is earmarked for people living in the Age of Aquarius? Where is this knowledge for humankind that may provide the intelligence-energy to mentally control and direct the motion and circumstances of the whole of our universe? What, if any, cosmic bonds already exist that may unite our universe and its inhabitants with the Heavens above, which contain the potential of all mass and all time? Even beginnings or ends of terrestrial entities are merely changes in the cycles of our universe or results of other cosmic changes that have profound and sometimes irreversible effects on each other. Because of the essential limitations of the rational mind, we have to accept the fact that scientific ideas and theories have a limited range in their description of reality.

After all, has any segment of the scientific community created something that had no prior existence? When physicists extended the range of their probing into the unfamiliar subatomic realm of reality, they were confronted with the realization that most of their fundamental frames of reference were in need of revision. They could no longer deal with approximate and limited views of universal reality. Just as we urgently need to change our attitude towards achieving a deeper understanding of the world around us, our value system also requires careful reexamination, which must, of necessity, bring about far-reaching changes in our society. The ultimate question still remaining for us to grapple with is simply this: Where is this body of knowledge, if it does in fact exist, that we may draw from to meet and achieve our objective of turning ultimate destruction to everlasting and eternal peace and tranquility?

In your compendium, Rav Shimon bar Yochai, which is the Book of Splendor—the Zohar—shall Israel in the future taste from the Tree of Life, and the world shall go forth from its exile with mercy.[60]

The future is here and now. Kabbalah connection awaits us all for those who merely extend a welcome hand.

Rav Chiya said, "In the days of Rav Shimon bar Yochai, even the birds utter wisdom, for his words are known Above and Below." Rav Chiya then quoted the verse: "And God said to Moses, 'Behold thou shall sleep with thy fathers.'" (Deuteronomy 31:16) "Mark this," he said. "As long as Moses was alive, he used to check Israel from sinning. And because Moses was among them, there shall not be a generation like that one till the days of the Messiah. How much more those who stand before Rav Shimon and learn from him, and how very much more Rav Shimon himself, who is above all! Alas for the world when Rav Shimon shall depart, and the fountains of wisdom shall be closed, and men shall seek wisdom and there will be none to impart it, and the Bible will be interpreted erroneously because there will be none who is acquainted with wisdom!" Said Rav Yehuda, "God will one day reveal the hidden mysteries of the Bible, namely, at the time of the Messiah, because 'the Earth shall be full of the knowledge of the Lord like the waters cover the sea' (Isaiah 11:9) and as it is written: 'They shall teach no more every man his neighbor or every man his brother, saying, Know the Lord (Tetragrammaton), for they shall all know Me from the smallest to the greatest of them.' (Jeremiah 31:34)"

Many of the challenging topics discussed in science today, especially the nature of black holes, the consequences of gravitational collapse, and the early stages of the Big Bang, present science with a crisis unparalleled in history. Progress in science had become so commonplace that most people have accepted it as a natural process of the interpretation of nature. For centuries now, we have assumed that however abstruse an aspect of nature may appear, science will always find the answer. Only recently—in fact, only in the past few decades—has the scientific community come to the realization that we are faced with a bewildering and confusing array of complex life forms that is failing to adequately cope with the new physics. On the other hand, the deeper our probing, the simpler the task will become, and we shall stand on the threshold of a whole new era of physics.

The route to the new physics of the future lies beyond the dimension of the physical reality of our world. It will permit us to go beyond space-time in our analysis, until hopefully, a door will open one day, a door no wider than the eye of a needle, and unto us shall open the Supernal Gates exposing the glittering interrelatedness of the universe with all its beauty and simplicity.[61] Toward the arrival of that date, the *Zohar* holds out more hope than does science, which must rely largely on randomness and probability. *The Book of Splendor* intends to provide a direct link to and contact with the universal energy-intelligence that we discussed previously and subsequently present the world of metaphysics as an exact, simplified science. The new science of Kabbalah does indeed answer many of the enigmatic aspects of nature, yet still it remains elegantly simple. The new physics of Kabbalah and Einsteinian classical physics may be brought into agreement by a better understanding of what each represents through its particular frames of reference. The *Zohar*'s world view of our universe transcends and occupies a frame beyond space-time, whereas modern physics remains fixed and limited to such frames of reference as presented by Einstein.

The new kabbalistic vision of reality that we have been talking about is based on an in-depth perception of the Bible's coded narrations and tales. The description provided by the Bible sounds quite similar to the description of modern space systems, emphasizing, as it does, the outer-space connection as the energy-intelligence system referred to as the Tree of Life.

The *Zohar*[62] explains:

> *"And Moses was one hundred and twenty years."* / 20
> (Deuteronomy 31:16) *This is an allusion to Moses, through whose agency the Law was given and who bestowed life on man from the Tree of Life. And in truth, had Israel not sinned [with the golden calf], they would have been proof against death, since the Tree of Life had been brought down to them.... Hence we have learned Moses did not die, but he was gathered in from this world and caused the moon to shine, being in this respect like the sun, which also after setting does not expire but gives light to the moon.*
>
> *Rav Elazar said, "God will one day re-establish the world and strengthen the spirit of the sons of men so that they may prolong their days forever, as it is written: 'For as the days of a tree so shall be the days of my people, etc.' (Isaiah 65:22)".*

Did Moses die? Is he actually still alive? When Moses was 120 years old, he was told by God to go up unto the mountains of Moab: "and the Lord buried him in the land of Moab, but no man knows of his sepulcher unto this day." (*Deuteronomy* 34:6) Is it conceivable that his body did not remain on Earth but was transported ("gathered") by a space vehicle to outer space (Heaven)? The *Zohar* states that, incredible as it may seem, Moses did not die. His cosmic bond with the outer-space connection, the Tree of Life, was never severed as had been the case with the Israelites after the golden calf incident. Had the Israelites not sinned, their cosmic connection with the Tree of Life would have remained eternally and their days on earth "prolonged forever," states the *Zohar*.

What is the significance of the *Zoharic* comparison of Moses to the sun?

Like everyone else, I have been curious enough to ask whether there really is extraterrestrial life on other planets or elsewhere. As an increasing number of scientists search for evidence either of extraterrestrial intelligence or whether any of these extraterrestrials ever visited Earth on some kind of transport system, the more I am slowly coming to the conclusion that the answer may rest with the possibility that has already been alluded to in both the Bible and the *Zohar*. Preposterous as it may seem and despite the lack of hard evidence to support the existence of extraterrestrial life, a number of scientists are becoming increasingly vocal about its possibility, not to mention the popular recognition and acceptance given, in spite of the statistical evidence against it.

Before proceeding to explore and interpret the *Zoharic* account of the death of Moses, I would like to relate another account of biblical space transportation, one very similar to the startling pattern recorded in Deuteronomy but which most probably has been overlooked by most of us because of our educational mental programming.

And Elijah took his mantle, wrapped it together, and smote the waters and they were divided, so that the two of them went over on dry ground.... And it came to pass, as they still went on and talked that, behold, there appeared a chariot of fire and horses of fire, and parted them from one another; and Elijah went up by a whirlwind into Heaven. Elisha saw it and cried, "My father, my father, the chariot of Israel and the horsemen." And he saw him no more. (2 Kings 2:8-12)

The striking similarities between these two biblical accounts—the characteristics of the paranormal phenomena, the possibility of space travel, and the presentation of eternal life—will hopefully provide a framework for understanding and communication data, as well as a basis for gaining insight into our universe. It now appears far more complex and bewildering than was suspected a mere two decades ago. It is clear that the present scientific world view of our universe is still in its infancy, but the quest for unification and interrelatedness has become one of the principal areas of investigation in modern physics. Perhaps explaining all of nature in terms of a single unified energy-intelligence will ultimately be realized. Our investigation of biblical phenomena will take us along a path of physical laws presently unknown to us, but utilized by Moses and Elijah.

Even a modest attempt to review all of the facets mentioned in these two accounts would burst the frame of a book much larger than this one. Consequently, I shall address and limit my inquiry to the energy-intelligence known as the Tree of

Life, space transportation, and eternal life, which appears in our subject material.

Moses and Elijah were observed leaving Earth. Elisha describes the space transport as a chariot of fire with horses of fire, something that sounds very similar to the exhaust of a modern-day rocket engine. The *Zohar* states that Moses did not die but that his body was transported to Heaven, in similar fashion to that recorded by Elisha. Moses' body was not seen after his death. These two prophets were again seen alive when they appeared before Rav Shimon bar Yochai and his son. Rav Elazar in the cave of Pequi'in where the revelation of the *Zohar* took place.[63] In the seclusion of the cave, Rav Shimon was visited twice a day by the prophet Elijah, who revealed to him the secrets of the *Zohar*. Its deeper and more comprehensive sections, known as the *Ra'ya Mehemna* (Faithful Shepherd), are a record of the discourses that took place between Rav Shimon and Moses himself, the beloved shepherd.

These meetings took place hundreds of years after Moses' and Elijah's departure from the Earth. How was this possible, and by what means was it accomplished?

The cloud or chariot, their space vehicle transport, was continually with them, either for their journey to outer space or their return to Earth. The universal energy-intelligence force was making contact with Rav Shimon and his son Rav Elazar through the extraterrestrial Moses and Elijah. Rav Shimon had made contact with the outer-space connection, the Tree of Life, which Adam had been connected to before the Fall.

The connection of Moses and Elijah to the Tree of Life would remain eternal. Consequently, they could not nor would ever meet the inevitable finale of all flesh: Death. They did not die but remained as the sun, which after setting does not expire or "die" but gives light to the moon, as portrayed so beautifully by the *Zohar*[64]. Indeed, according to the Bible and the *Zohar*, extraterrestrial righteous individuals have always been instrumental in helping humankind on this earth.

> *And it came to pass when Joshua was by Jericho, that he lifted up his eyes and looked and there stood a man against him with sword drawn in his hand. Joshua went to him and said to him, "Are you for or against us?" And he said, "No, I come before you as captain of the Host of the Lord." Joshua fell on his face to the earth and worshipped, saying, "What says my Lord to His servant?" And the captain of the Lord's Host said to Joshua, "Remove your shoe from off your foot, for the place where you are standing is sacred." Joshua did so.*

> *And the Lord said to Joshua, "See, I have given into your hand Jericho, and its king and mighty men of valor."*

> *Joshua, the son of Nun, called the Priests and said unto them, "Take up the Ark of the Covenant and let seven Priests bear seven sounding horns before the Ark of the Lord." (Joshua 5:13-15; 6:2-6)*

The rest is biblical history. "The captain of the host of the Lord," an extraterrestrial individual, came to the assistance of Joshua and the Israelites by providing the system by which a cosmic connection to the energy-intelligence force, the Tree of Life, could be achieved. The Ark of the Covenant, which played so important a role in Israel's conquest of the Holy Land, served as a space station through which the energy-intelligence force would become manifest. The loss of the Ark in later years spelled doom for the Israelites. But during the time of this story, "the walls of Jericho came tumbling down."

This was the same Ark of the Covenant that had been carried by the Israelites during their 40 years of wandering through the Sinai wilderness. "You shall put into the Ark the Testimony [Bible], which I shall give you." (*Exodus* 25:16) Instilled with extraterrestrial intelligence by virtue of its eternal cosmic connection to the Tree of Life, this same Ark was instrumental in many miraculous, paranormal events during the time of King David.

> *And when they came to Nachon's threshing floor, Uzzah put forth his hand to the Ark of the Lord and took hold of it, for the oxen shook it. And the anger of the Lord was kindled against Uzzah; and the Lord (the Tetragrammaton) smote him there for his error and he died by the Ark of the Lord.* (*2* Samuel 6:6-7)

The Ark contained an incredible degree of cosmic energy force, so powerful that it struck down Uzzah and he died on the spot.

The celestial struggle at the Red Sea was a marvelous spectacle that has not been forgotten. Mentioned in numerous verses throughout the Bible, it was an unusual event, and because it was so unusual, it has remained as one of the most impressive cosmic upheavals in the long history of the humanity.

> *And Moses stretched out his hand over the sea, and the Lord caused the sea to go back by a strong east wind all that night, and made the sea dry land, and the waters were divided.* (*Exodus* 14:21)

All nations and peoples of the world experienced this enormous cosmic energy-intelligence force that instantly pervaded the entire universe, according to the biblical commentator Rashi and as explained by the *Mehilta* 14:21 (Hebrew commentary on the *Book of Exodus* produced by a Talmudic School founded by Ishmael ben Elisha *circa*. A.D. 300 and known as the House of Ishmael): "The waters of all oceans and seas were divided."

Rav Ashlag, in his book *Tree of Life* stated: "A unified energy force at work with no beginning or end, itself eternal as the cosmic present and flowing equally without relation to anything external was the cosmic power force tapped by Moses." Moses provided a connection for the children of Israel that would control the flow of the water at a molecular level, forming it into two vertical walls.

A cosmic upheaval of such proportions swept through every corner of the Earth and universe, and the traditions of many peoples as well as the cosmological myth persist that seas were torn apart: "Waters were piled up to the height of sixteen hundred miles and they could be seen by all the nations of the world." (*Targum Yerushalmi, Exodus* 14:22) This peculiar demonstration in which Moses drew the all-inclusive positive cosmic energy force by tapping the source of this energy from the Tree of Life gives us a futuristic panorama of the new physical laws of nature.

Scientists today are discovering a whole array of new phenomena, many of which have taken us from the familiar material world, which belongs to human experience, to a signpost pointing to a more complex view of reality. Time and space, objectively speaking, have almost vanished in the paranormal, in the worlds of metaphysics, along a path strewn with paradoxes and strange phenomena. These biblical incidents all suggest concepts and things that will hopefully be rediscovered, leading eventually to a redefinition of reality in a way that all mankind can see and understand.

The journey pursued in these pages has been an attempt to track down the cosmic power sources of our universe, and once the cosmic connection has been bonded, to embark on a journey toward unity with the Father of our universe, the all-embracing Unity of energy-intelligence.

The applied science of cosmic energy was again demonstrated by the prophet Elijah when he parted the waters of the Jordan. Elijah, having made his connection with the Tree of Life energy force, intervened in the physical affairs of matter with fantastic phenomena and strange descriptions. The links that do exist between the scientific and the apparently paranormal are presented in biblical verses as demonstrations that the world around us of seemingly unconnected yet interrelated events is merely a manifestation of an all-embracing whole.

The course of the all-inclusive positive energy force, the Light of Wisdom—to provide mankind with the knowledge and intelligence to reconcile the finite with the infinite— was left to Moses and Elijah. As extraterrestrial personalities, they were destined to transmit the knowledge and application of the Tree of Life, which emerges as the *Zohar*, the *Book of Splendor*. Celestial mechanics will no longer conflict with cosmic reality. If the activity in an atom constitutes the paradigm for the physical world, then the biblical events are not merely accidents of celestial movement but occurrences as normal as birth and death. Links between the extraterrestrial and our physical universe are no longer limited to the domain of human perception.

The world of metaphysics has become closely aligned with the world of physical reality all around us. Taking this point to its extreme, let us explore the power of mind waves that, within the foreseeable future, will become detectable with improved scientific instruments. I refer to a cosmic intelligence force that can be directed at will. As life in space becomes less of an adventure and takes on the trappings of the routine, future wars may very well be waged in space— precisely because the very depths of space will have become as familiar to us as our own backyard, which has served and continues to serve as a playground for human suffering and war-torn destruction. Opposing space-satellite armadas, like their airborne counterparts of another time, will be trading fire with each other in a zero-dimension confrontation. In anticipation of wars in which enemy planes and satellites will be traveling at speeds faster than the speed of light, speed computer techniques will be developed that can quickly indicate the most effective response to an enemy threat. Artificial intelligence systems will handle decision-making, and all that will be left to the human defense command is the pushing of a button. The battle should not take more than a few minutes before victor and vanquished are determined.

Science fiction? Well, let us explore the first instance of Star Wars, directed not by computers but by actual physical energy signals created by the thought process as a brain wave.

We read in the *Zohar*[65]:

> *And Balak the son of Tzipor saw all that Israel had done to the Amorites.* (Numbers 22:2) *What did he see? He saw both through the window of wisdom and with his physical eyes. There is one window through which the very essence of wisdom can be seen. He was the "son of a bird" [tzipor, in English, means "bird"], for he used birds for all his metaphysical arts... The bird would come to him and tell him certain things... One day, Balak did his usual thing with the bird and it flew away, never to return. He was greatly*

distressed, and then he saw it coming with a fiery
flame following it and burning its wings... This was
the thinking process of Moses, generating fiery energy
against the Amorites in Heshbon. "For there is a fire
gone out of Heshbon, a flame from the city of Sihon:
It has consumed Ar of Moab, and the lords of the high
places of Arnon." (Numbers 21:28)

The tapping of this energy by Moses permitted the energy-intelligence force, through mental effort, to control the molecular motion of the bird's wing, thereby preventing it from flying.[66]

Mind control of this nature was at one time a principle reserved for only a select few kabbalists. However, in the Age of Aquarius, "all mankind shall know." (*Jeremiah* 31:33) Mind control, whereby thought processes can control the movement of molecules, was used during the Great *Exodus*. More specifically, this procedure is demonstrated today during the *Pesach* Seder when the three matzot are designated Kohen, Levi, and Israel. While for the present, the direction of an atom being controlled by our thought processes cannot be scientifically detected, the sages of the *Haggadah* suggested this tripartite designation of the *matzot*, whereby they provided the Israelite with both the knowledge and method by which mind power would move the infinite atoms within the *matzot*, thereby achieving a cosmic connection with the all-inclusive positive energy-intelligence. This energy-intelligence produces for the individual on *Pesach* a personal *Exodus* from bondage, that freedom from the Desire to Receive for Oneself Alone that so few of us ever experience. The mental designation of one *matzah* as Kohen (where the *matzah*, which just a few seconds before was in a box together with all the other matzot, now assumes another dimension of cosmology: Kohen) temporarily changes the characteristic of the *matzah*, inserting one's own energy force, rearranging the *matzah*'s molecules so that the positive, Right Column force of the atom becomes the dominant molecule of the *matzah*, which is now referred to as the "Kohen *matzah* of positive domination." The same procedure continues for the second *matzah* in which the dominant molecule is becomes the negative or Left Column force: Levi. Finally, the third *matzah* becomes the dominant energy force of the Central Column or the neutron, and is designated as Israel.

Consequently, if we were to ask ourselves whether man will progress to a sufficiently high level to make use of mind over matter and thereby make the connection with the Tree of Life, the outer-space connection, my answer would be in the affirmative, inasmuch as this phenomenon has already been demonstrated by an entire nation: The Israelites during the Great *Exodus*.

I would be remiss if I closed this chapter without mentioning one of the serious outcomes of our newly established phenomenon of mind exerting molecular control over matter. With this control, it is very likely that *Homo sapiens* will one day fly without the use of aircraft, spacecraft or any other physical means of transportation. Legend provides us with numerous accounts of flights by Elijah, Rav Shimon, and Rav Isaac Luria, whereby they rose into the air and travelled from Galilee to Jerusalem. This brings us to an account recorded in the *Zohar*[67], which, I must confess, is probably the most fascinating, incredible, yet actual account of human flight through space ever recorded.

Rav Elazar said, "Who killed the wicked Balaam and how was he killed?" Rav Yitzchak replied, "Pinchas and his comrades killed him, as it says: 'They slew on their slain.' (Numbers 31:8) We have learned that through his magic arts, he and the kings of Midian were able to fly in the air. And it was the Holy Diadem (Exodus 29:6) of the High Priest and the meditation of Pinchas that brought them down 'on their slain.'" Said Rav Elazar, "I know all this."

Rav Shimon then said, "Elazar, Balaam was a powerful adversary, as it says: 'There arose not a prophet in Israel like Moses,' but there did arise among other nations, to wit, Balaam, (Deuteronomy 34:10) who was supreme among the Lower Crowns [lower frame of reference of energy-intelligence; lesser mind control of the atom] as Moses was among the Upper Crowns [higher level of energy-intelligence control].

"How then were they able to kill him? The answer lies in a remark from the Book of Wisdom of King Solomon. There are three signs in a man [the level of intelligence-energy mind control is determined by and dependent upon three signs of a man's character]: Paleness is a sign of anger, talking is a sign of folly,

and self-praise is a sign of ignorance. It is true that it says: 'Let a stranger praise you and not your own mouth,' (Proverbs 27:2) and we alter this to 'Let a stranger praise you.' But the wicked Balaam praised himself in everything, and deceived people as well. He made much of little [consequently, his egocentricity prevented him from achieving a higher altered state of consciousness]. For all that he said of himself referred only to the unclean grades. Though it was true, it did not mean much. Though whoever heard it imagined that he surpassed all the prophets of the world."

We have raised the question as to whether humankind can sufficiently elevate itself to a spiritual level of altered consciousness connecting with the outer-space connection, the Tree of Life, and subsequently control their bodies by thought or molecular motion in a way that ultimately leads to the ability to fly. The *Zohar* and the Bible provide factual accounts of mankind controlling matter in the same manner as we mentally control our limbs and other parts of our physical body. The possibility of man achieving the ability to fly without the use of the physical means of transportation already existed when humankind had progressed to the level of cosmic connection to the Tree of Life, the link to the outer-space connection. Using and abusing such powers selfishly, as did Balaam, was accompanied by a decline and the ultimate disintegration and general loss of harmony among *Homo sapiens*, which inevitably led to the outbreak of universal disruption and discord.

During the painful process of discord, however, the ability to maintain a cosmic bond to the outer-space connection was not completely lost. Although the mainstream of our society experienced a decline in the level of spirituality, a small minority of spiritual people has always appeared on the scene and carried on the knowledge of universal intelligence. The scientific transformation we are now experiencing, both in depth and magnitude, suggests a need for a complete reexamination of our basic world view of the universe, and hopefully, a re-conceptualizing of basic concepts leading to a holistic framework of our physical reality.

Let us now return to the *Zohar*[68] for an incredible account of possible future warfare that, from a kabbalistic view, may be prevented from taking place.

> *Now where was Balaam at that time? Seeing that he said, "Now I am going to my people," (Numbers 24:14) how can he have been in Midian? The truth is that when he saw that 24,000 Israelites perished by his counsel, he stayed there and demanded his reward; and while he was staying there, Pinchas and his captains of the hosts came there. When Balaam saw Pinchas, he flew up into the air with his two sons Yunus and Yumburus. But these two, you will say, died at the time when the golden calf was made...*

> *In fact, with their supernatural powers, they produced a living golden calf. (Exodus 32:1-6) Balaam, however, being acquainted with every kind of witchcraft took also those of his sons, and began to fly*

away. When Pinchas saw a man in the air flying away, he shouted to his soldiers, "Is anyone able to fly after him, for it is Balaam?" Then Zilya, of the tribe of Dan, arose and seized the root source of energy of the dominion of witchcraft, the power that rules over all extensions of sorcery and witchcraft, and flew after him. When Balaam saw him, he changed his direction in the air [warp nine] and broke through five levels of galaxies and vanished from view. Zilya was then sorely vexed, not knowing what to do. Pinchas called out after tapping the connection of the Tree of Life and ordered the Ruler of the cosmic dragons, which overshadow all serpents, to sever all infusion of cosmic power to Balaam. The metaphysical command by Pinchas brought Balaam into view, whereupon Zilya approached him and brought him down in front of Pinchas....

When Balaam came down in front of him, Pinchas said to him, "Wretch, how many evil happenings have you brought upon the holy people?" Pinchas then said to Zilya, "Kill him, but not with the Cosmic Name, for it is not fitting that Balaam meet his fate by the Divine sanctity of the Holy Name." The reason for this is to prevent his [Balaam's] soul, when leaving him, from becoming united with higher levels of spiritual, holy cosmic energy forces, and his prayer [be] fulfilled: "May my soul die the death of the righteous." (Numbers 23:10) He [Zilya] then tried to kill him in many ways, but did not succeed until he [Zilya] took a sword on which was engraved a snake on each side.

*Pinchas said, "Kill him with his own weapon." And
then he did kill him; for such is the way of that side;
he who follows it is killed by it, and it is with his soul
when it departs from him.* ~spirit~

One who lives by and connects with cosmic negative energy
forces ultimately meets death at the hand of this very same
energy force, inasmuch as cosmic negative energy is an
intelligence-energy force, the same as the all-inclusive
positive cosmic force. As an intelligence-energy force, a
negative cosmic force has no purpose or direction except to
heap destruction on whatever comes into contact with it. It
is the kind of robot that does not learn to be selective in its
objective, and if turned toward its master can successfully
annihilate the very essence and cause of its own existence. If
an employer teaches his employee how to steal from his
competition, that very same employee will one day turn
around and steal from his teacher. The innate characteristic
of positive energy is to extend outward and to duplicate the
cause of its essence, which is one of sharing, whereas
negative energy tends to turn inward, which is the aspect of
the Desire to Receive, without regard to other entities.

The difficulty in maintaining the concept of "love thy
neighbor as thy self" (*Leviticus* 19:18) in our society lies
precisely in our inability to accept the presence of others.
First and foremost, is the self, guided by a cosmic energy-
intelligence of negativity, which is a universal problem. The
price that humankind pays for its link to cosmic negativity
is far too high, and we can ill afford to continue in our
present state of human suffering. The principle of cause and

effect dictates the life process of our universe. This is why Pinchas recognized the necessity of using the same cosmic weapon in ridding the world of so powerful a negative individual as Balaam.

The past ten years have taught us to be cautious with the word "impossible." The possibility of human travel beyond our own solar system is a staggering realization, albeit a concept that most of us do not really expect to come about in our lifetime. The fundamental problem lies in inadequate propulsion that seems to have limited humankind to our planet. Alternative methods are necessary to reduce time travel to figures compatible with our life span. Consequently, travel speeds necessary to meet this requirement would have to approach or exceed the speed of light.

The *Zohar* apparently does not consider the problems connected with approaching the speed of light as the obstacle to achieving human travel beyond our solar system, inasmuch as the problem does not lie in producing the infinite speed required to accelerate an object beyond the speed of light barrier. The crisis facing the scientist today is Einstein's theory of relativity, which has withstood the test of critical experiment and which indicates that the speed of an object can approach infinity only when the object approaches the speed of light—and it is impossible to exceed the speed of light.

Amazingly enough, the *Zohar* presents a plan that will provide man with the capability of turning the entire solar system, including terrestrial Earth, into a human backyard, in much the same way that the airplane converted the once-formidable oceans into little more than swimming holes.

The solution lies, not in producing a means of propulsion that will break through the speed of light barrier, but rather in simply *removing the barrier itself.* This concept has been hinted at in many accounts recorded in both the Bible and the *Zohar.* Strange as this may sound, it is all in perfect harmony with the New Age ideas concerning the laws of space and time. There is no fundamental reason why the world of physics cannot create a new renaissance that will open up the whole solar system to humankind transportation as stated in the *Zohar*[69]. No new revolutionary discoveries are really required because Einstein's apparent proof that we cannot drive starships faster than the speed of light is not and should not be considered as the only real obstacle in the future.

The answer, as clearly and simply stated in the *Zohar*[70], is that the removal of the *light barrier* depends completely upon the removal of the *humankind* barrier represented by hate and intolerance of each other. This feat of overcoming the obstacles of space travel and the light barrier was clearly demonstrated by both the prophet Elijah and Pinchas, who were actually one and the same person, albeit during different lifetimes.

Both Elijah and Pinchas knew and understood where to look in the hazy forest of light barriers and thus knew how to dissect the anatomy of interstellar flight.

In summary, with our present scientific knowledge, we should be able to respond to the challenge of interstellar space exploration by recognizing the formidable obstacle that stands in our way: Ignoring the concept of "love thy neighbor as thyself."

The kabbalistic world view of essential reality reflects the innate harmonious interrelatedness of our universe. To achieve a state of dynamic balance, a cultural revolution will be needed. The dissipation of the light barrier in particular—and, I might add, the survival of our entire galaxy—may very well depend on whether we can bring about a unified wholeness of mankind. The removal of physical barriers depends completely on our ability to remove our metaphysical barriers of intolerance and hatred. The universe can no longer be viewed as a machine consisting of a multitude of physical objects, but must be seen instead as one dynamic whole where non-physical entities, such as thought processes and the nature of consciousness are essentially part of and related to the universal whole.

Furthermore, metaphysical manifestations are always the primary reality and essence, which manifest themselves ultimately as a web of material, physical patterns. To be more precise, it is the manifestation of thought that precedes the emergence of material patterns. The world must be viewed as a complicated web of infinite events, material and non-material, that determine the tissue of the whole.

Then, and only then, can we understand the dynamic interplay of our cosmos, where, in the kabbalistic world view of cosmic reality, the conceptual issue of tolerance may be the all-important factor in determining the substance of the whole. And cosmic consciousness and astral influences are very much a part of the universal thread of our cosmic order.

*"THE ONLY CONSTANT PHENOMENON OF
CIVILIZATION IS CHANGE."*

—Anonymous

CHAPTER TWELVE

THE REVOLUTION OF CHANGE

Tradition is a respectable word but it no longer has any place in the lexicon of science, finance or government. Just as we are in the throes of a world-wide revolution in communication systems, international cooperation, and social reforms, we find examples that are all too familiar of how seriously repressive long-established patterns of thought can be. Technology, especially electronics, is becoming obsolete at an ever-increasing rate. The science of physics has emerged as an uncertainty principle. Change is inevitable.

The only constant known to mankind is change.

Interestingly enough, the revolving wheel of change never seems to come to an end, and the economic and social burdens resulting from the ending of an old cycle of life must be balanced with the enormous weight of the unknown that comes with a new cycle. We seem to be at a critical crossroad where meaning and significance have little to offer by way of gaining an understanding of how to be one with the universe. The rapid rate of change, both social and economic, in the past 20 years has created a state of imbalance, resulting in the breaking down of family, traditions, and cultural values.

There is a striking parallel between the dramatic changes brought about by the microchip to the electronic and computer industries and the disastrous disorder experienced from environmental pollution and the widespread use of drugs. Both have dramatically increased man's alienation from himself, his environment, and his culture. The former has almost reduced the initiative of man to a robotic consciousness, while the latter has thrust man into a feeling of isolation and an inability to communicate with his fellows. Miniaturization in technology has brought a greater awareness of the internal, subatomic level of interrelatedness, while social and moral disintegration has strengthened the hand of isolation, where time-proven values and moral standards, which were once supportive of relationships, are crumbling and becoming meaningless to our society as a whole. Curiously though, the interrelatedness of humankind appears to be running a course quite contrary to the internal field of inanimate matter, which, with our advancing technological progress, continues to point to an interrelatedness of the all-embracing unity.

Many sociologists and government planners have expressed deep concern about our inability to respond properly, should the continuing disintegration of our social structure trigger the need for a dramatic increase in social welfare. Some of the issues we are facing are the high rate of unemployment and a higher incidence of the divorce rate. This is the key issue among many, relating to the deeper needs of man, no matter how much comfort the material sciences may give to the physical body.

Does change hold lessons for mankind? What is lacking is a proper sense of perspective, of the real contribution that modern technology as a whole has made to human well-being. At the same time, there is a failure to understand that change cannot always perform miracles and that the inevitable risks that must accompany change must also be accepted. It is perhaps too much to ask of ourselves that we strike a balance, inasmuch as we have conditioned ourselves to demand the best for our material needs without necessarily considering the responsibilities that such change may entail.

All of this poses a serious problem for the science of astrology. Traditionally, the search for the cosmic connection was left to astrologers and consequently has been dismissed as superstition by the scientific community. One difficulty relates to the discovery of three new planets: Uranus in 1781, Neptune in 1846, and Pluto in 1930. Because of these discoveries, conventional astrology recently has undergone changes. Aries and Scorpio were once ruled by Mars, but Scorpio is now considered a cosmic entity under Pluto, and Pisces is now governed by Neptune. Saturn, that "Old Father Time" planet, once considered the cosmic ruler of Capricorn and Aquarius, was also subject to a change; and we find the sign Aquarius ruled by Uranus.

From a kabbalistic view of our universe, these three "newly" discovered planets will not in any way change the course of astral influences that have been established from its very inception. It is only when we treat a planet from its outward, external cosmic energy aspect that we tend to believe that with its discovery greater awareness and greater recognition of the astral influences of planets by man take place.

> Rav Shimon said, "I raised my head in prayer to the Supernal Whole, that the wisdom of Kabbalah be revealed by me within the terrestrial lower world as it was concealed within my heart. We do not make use of the external knowledge, but rather the in-depth sublime path of the coded Bible is our source reference. The seven planetary bodies that are in constant motion, which are referred to by names of a lower, external dimension, namely, Saturn, Jupiter, Mars, Sun, Venus, Mercury, and the Moon are symbolic and directed by its seven internal cosmic influences, which are concealed from the knowledge of conventional astrology. These seven astral forces are the seven Sefirot of Mercy, Judgment, Beauty, Victory, Splendor, Foundation, and Kingdom. The internal energy force does not undergo any changes. The external body energy force is subjected to change and consequently creates confusion in its physical expression."[71]

The language and knowledge of astrology will not undergo any change along with the usual progressive change in human and technological development. What emerges from human progress, as well as technological development, is merely to permit us to grow with greater consciousness, to become more aware of the existence and validity of the laws and principles established by either conventional astrology or kabbalistic astrology. But kabbalistic astrology is not subject to new discoveries because the root of its development has already been known since the time of Abraham. Consequently, any new revelations and new manifestations will in no way affect the astral influences taking place in our universe. If changes are taking place, they are taking place because the celestial bodies are taking on new positions, and these positions are merely for the observation of those changes that may be taking place on the manifested, external physical level.

Our concern and the objective of this book is to make certain that negative cosmic energies do not exercise the kind of influence that they have in the past. With the dawning of the Age of Aquarius and as we move closer to a more universal humanitarian relationship, the sciences will begin to recognize the more subtle, internal interrelationships between man and the cosmos. As the internal relationships between man evolve and become more fully developed, so will more of the invisible world become visible to science and the ultimate interrelationship be seen at its sub-cosmic level.

ADDITIONAL INFORMATION ABOUT CONCEPTS DISCUSSED IN THE BOOK

THE TWELVE TRIBES OF ISRAEL AND THE TREE OF LIFE

We have learned that biblical narrative is the outer covering for many inner levels of concealed truths. An example of this is the story of Jacob and his twelve sons, who became the leaders of the twelve tribes of Israel. The chariot of the *Sefira* of Tiferet contains six *Sefirot*: *Chesed, Gevurah, Tiferet, Netzach, Hod,* and *Yesod.* Each of these *Sefirot,* in its male and female aspect, can be attributed to one of the twelve sons, to the twelve months of the year, and to their astrological signs. Of the remaining four *Sefirot* (*Keter, Chochmah, Binah, Malchut*), the Upper Three have no direct influence on this mundane level of existence, while *Malchut* represents the Desire to Receive—man himself, who is the ultimate recipient of all these energies.

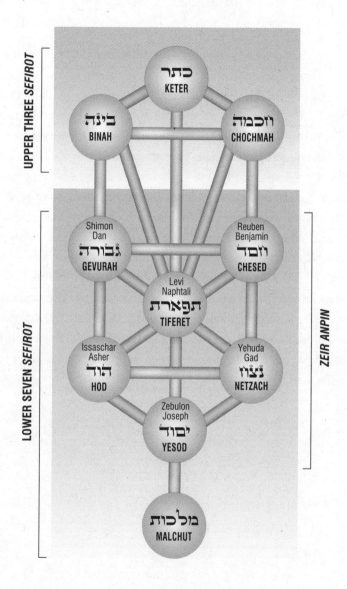

THE SHIELD OF DAVID

The Shield of David, in a broader sense, implies the concept of cosmic consciousness. When a thorough knowledge of the Upper and Lower Triads has been achieved then one can reach a *Devekut* with the cosmos which is represented by the Shield of David. Cosmic influences, namely the seven basic planets together with the twelve signs of the Zodiac, are directly related and bound up with the above seven *Sefirot*. Each *Sefirah* is considered the internal energy of the seven planets which are as follows: Saturn, Jupiter, Mars, Sun, Venus, Mercury and the Moon, in this order. Each planet rules over and dominates two signs of the Zodiac. The Sun and Moon rule over only one sign. Through Kabbalistic Meditation, one can connect with cosmic consciousness thereby achieving a level of pure awareness. When the individual has mastered the art of direct communion with and an attachment to the inner aspect of these cosmic influences, the *Sefirot*, then it is the individual who can now direct his destiny.

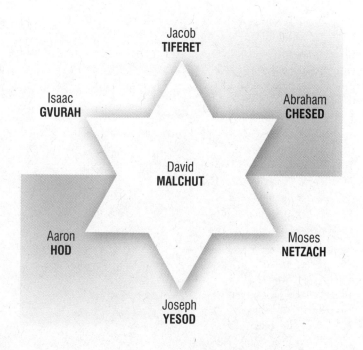

ZOHAR FOOTNOTES

1   *Zohar* Terumah 831-832
2   *Zohar* Toldot 3
3   *Zohar* Toldot 3
4   *Zohar* Toldot 3
5   *Zohar* Noach 252-253, *Zohar* Beresheet B 311
6   *Zohar* Toldot 3
7   *Zohar* Toldot 3
8   *Zohar* Emor 141
9   *Zohar* Ki Tetze 113
10 *Zohar* Terumah 831-860, *Zohar* Vayakhel 159
11 *Zohar* Vayakhel 158-161
12 *Zohar* Shemot 75-111
13 *Zohar* Shemot 105-161
14 *Zohar* Shemot 157-161
15 *Zohar* Ki Tetze 113
16 *Zohar* Miketz 50-51
17 *Zohar* Miketz 50-51
18 *Zohar* Ki Tisa 60-63
19 *Zohar* Vayeshev 30-35
20 *Zohar* Ki Tetze 113
21 *Zohar* Emor 250
22 *Zohar* Ki Tetze 113
23 *Zohar* Chukkat 35-52
24 *Zohar* Miketz 50-52
25 *Zohar* Miketz 56
26 *Zohar* Miketz 238
27 *Zohar* Shemot 75-161
28 *Zohar* Lech Lecha 322
29 *Zohar* Terumah 835-836
30 *Zohar* Beresheet B 311
31 *Zohar* Terumah 837
32 *Zohar* Shlech Lecha 1-9
33 *Zohar* Terumah 837-841
34 *Zohar* Behar 58-62
35 *Zohar* Miketz 183
36 *Zohar* Miketz 186-188

37 *Zohar* Vayikra 239-244
38 *Zohar* Chayei Sarah 257-264
39 *Zohar* Beresheet 1
40 *Zohar* Bo 160-165
41 *Zohar* Bo 164-165
42 *Zohar* Bo 1-7
43 *Zohar* Vayera 476-483
44 *Zohar* Vayera 481
45 *Zohar* Vayera 481
46 *Zohar* Vayera 480-481
47 *Zohar* Vayera 480
48 *Zohar* Shemot 306-308
49 *Zohar* Vayera 250-255
50 *Zohar* Vayakhel 74-80
51 *Zohar* Beshalach 112
52 *Zohar* Beshalach 52
53 *Zohar* Noach 372-374
54 *Zohar* Chadash p. 39 sections 3-4
55 *Zohar* Chayei Sarah 34-36
56 *Zohar* Chayei Sarah 34-36
57 *Zohar* Beresheet B 356
58 *Zohar* Beresheet B 212
59 *Zohar* Beresheet A 472-474
60 *Zohar* Naso 90
61 *Zohar* Emor 129
62 *Zohar* Beresheet A 478-479, 482
63 Tikunei *Zohar* p. 1a
64 *Zohar* Beresheet A 479
65 *Zohar* Balak 1-2, 11
66 *Zohar* Balak 1-11
67 *Zohar* Balak 161-165
68 *Zohar* Balak 173-181
69 *Zohar* Balak 185
70 *Zohar* Ki Tetze 125
71 *Zohar* Ha'azinu 16-18

More from Rav Berg

Kabbalistic Astrology: And the Meaning of Our Lives
By Rav Berg

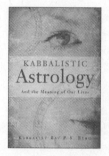

Discover your true nature and destiny, and how to shape it, through the power of Kabbalistic astrology. Much more than a book of horoscopes, *Kabbalistic Astrology* is a tool for understanding one's individual nature at its deepest level and putting that knowledge to immediate use in the real world. It explains why destiny is not the same as predestination; it teaches that we have many possible futures and can become masters of our fate.

Navigating the Universe: A roadmap for understanding the cosmic influences which shape our lives
By Rav Berg

Navigating the Universe offers a bridge between the earthly realm and the celestial realm, guiding us through illusion to the all embracing reality that the most fundamental natural laws date back to the heavens and its origins. According to kabbalistic principles, events on the earthly plane manifest as a result of cosmic influence. There are fundamentals such as astrology, time travel, and parallel universes that shape the human condition and exert their control over our physical universe. In this book, Rav Berg constructs a blueprint for those of us who are searching for total understanding of the world around us. By decoding biblical narratives, tales and parables of the Bible and *Zohar*, he shows that the roots of most misfortune can be traced to cosmic danger zones. He offers a precise timetable of celestial conditions so we can approach positive energy intelligences of the universe and tap their power. We're keyed into optimum times for undertaking a new venture such as opening a business, getting married, moving into a new home. Armed with this information, we can transcend the realm of chance, luck and indetermination.

More Ways to Bring the Wisdom of Kabbalah into Your Life

...To Be Continued...: Reincarnation & the Purpose of Our Lives
By Karen Berg

Reincarnation is the soul's journey back to the Light via multiple physical incarnations. In each lifetime, the soul returns to the physical world to correct a different aspect of itself. In one incarnation a soul may need to learn about being rich; another it may need to learn about being poor. Or it may need to experience strength and weakness, anger and compassion, beauty and unsightliness. Awareness of our soul's journey creates a context that helps us to guide our lives and appreciate what we were given. With this knowledge over many lifetimes our soul eventually manages to understand all the lessons and puts all of these fragments together. As it does so, the soul gathers sparks of Light back to itself. Eventually it returns to the source of all Light—the Creator—complete. When we understand reincarnation, our mistakes in this life don't become devastating. We develop a level of spiritual maturity that helps us to perceive how everything is part of a bigger plan designed to help us to change and grow. Death is not the end of the game, but just a chance to do over. We have nothing to fear. Life will be continued.

If You Don't Like Your Life, Change It!
By Yehuda Berg

It is possible to rise above the gravitational pull that draws us into the same scenes by using kabbalistic tools. Challenges such as pain, addiction and fear are opportunities for growth. By becoming familiar with underlying messages we tell ourselves, we can recognize and overcome destructive thoughts and reactive behavior, make different choices and ultimately create different results. Our decisions and actions today are seeds that create either chaos or fulfillment in our future.

When we step out of our nature, Nature responds in turn. According to the kabbalists that is how we can create miracles. Stop playing that old re-run! We all know we have the ability to transform; this book helps in understanding exactly what we need to change so we can rewrite our movie.

For those who loved *The Power of Kabbalah* or *Living Kabbalah*, get ready to take the next steps in writing, directing, and acting a new life.

On World Peace
By Rav Ashlag
Edited by Michael Berg

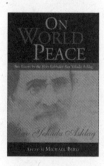

Everything that exists in reality, whether good or bad—including even the most evil and damage-causing thing in the world—has the right to exist, to the degree that destroying it and removing it completely from the world is forbidden. Rather, our duty is to only repair or fix it and to guide it towards goodness, for even a casual observation of any sort at the work of Creation that lies before us is enough [for us] to infer the high degree of perfection of Him Who has created it.

In these short but powerful treatises, Rav Ashlag explains that evil (or that which is not good), is nothing more than a work in progress and that seeing something as evil is no more relevant than judging an unripe fruit before it's time. He awakens us to the knowledge that upon arrival at our final destination *all things*, even the most damaged will be good.

This remarkable perspective helps us to view with awe the system the Creator has given us to develop and grow, and to gain certainty in the end of the journey. How will the process work? For this information, you'll want read the second essay, *One Precept* and experience for yourself the route to consciousness that Rav Ashlag so aptly charts out for us.

As the handwriting of a righteous person contains spiritual energy, *On World Peace* includes copies of Rav Ashlag's original writings. The book is nothing less than a gift to humanity.

The *Zohar*

Composed more than 2,000 years ago, the 23-volume *Zohar* is a commentary on biblical and spiritual matters written in the form of conversations among teachers. It was given to all humankind by the Creator to bring us protection, to connect us with the Creator's Light, and ultimately to fulfill our birthright of transformation. The *Zohar* is an effective tool for achieving our purpose in life.

More than eighty years ago, when The Kabbalah Centre was founded, the *Zohar* had virtually disappeared from the world. Today, all this has changed. Through the editorial efforts of Michael Berg, the *Zohar* is available in the original Aramaic language and for the first time in English with commentary.

We teach Kabbalah, not as a scholarly study but as a way of creating a better life and a better world.

WHO WE ARE

The Kabbalah Centre is a non-profit organization that makes the principles of Kabbalah understandable and relevant to everyday life. The Kabbalah Centre teachers provide students with spiritual tools based on kabbalistic principles that students can then apply as they see fit to improve their own lives and by doing so, make the world better. The Centre was founded by Rav Yehuda Ashlag in 1922 and now spans the globe with brick-and-mortar locations in more than 40 cities as well as an extensive online presence. To learn more, visit www.kabbalah.com.

WHAT WE TEACH

There are five core principles:

- **Sharing:** Sharing is the purpose of life and the only way to truly receive fulfillment. When individuals share, they connect to the force of energy that Kabbalah calls the Light—the Infinite Source of Goodness, the Divine Force, the Creator. By sharing, one can overcome ego—the force of negativity.

- **Awareness and Balance of the Ego:** The ego is a voice inside that directs people to be selfish, narrow-minded, limited, addicted, hurtful, irresponsible, negative, angry, and hateful. The ego is a main source of problems because it allows us to believe that others are separate from us. It is the opposite of sharing and humility. The ego also has a positive side, as it motivates one to take action. It is up to each individual to choose whether they act for themselves or whether to also act in the well-being of others. It is important to be aware of one's ego and to balance the positives and negatives.

- **Existence of Spiritual Laws:** There are spiritual laws in the universe that affect people's lives. One of these is the Law of

Cause and Effect: What one puts out is what one get back, or what we sow is what we reap.

- **We Are All One:** Every human being has within him- or herself a spark of the Creator that binds each and every person into one totality. This understanding informs us of the spiritual precept that every human being must be treated with dignity at all times, under any circumstances. Individually, everyone is responsible for war and poverty in all parts of the world and individuals can't enjoy true and lasting fulfillment as long as others are suffering.

- **Leaving Our Comfort Zone Can Create Miracles:** Becoming uncomfortable for the sake of helping others taps us into a spiritual dimension that ultimately brings Light and positivity to our lives.

HOW WE TEACH

Courses and Classes. On a daily basis, The Kabbalah Centre focuses on a variety of ways to help students learn the core kabbalistic principles. For example, The Centre develops courses, classes, online lectures, books, and audio products. Online courses and lectures are critical for students located around the world who want to study Kabbalah but don't have access to a Kabbalah Centre in their community.

Spiritual Services and Events. The Centre organizes and hosts a variety of weekly and monthly events and spiritual services where students can participate in lectures, meditation and share meals together. Some events are held through live streaming online. The Centre organizes spiritual retreats and tours to energy sites, which are places that have been closely touched by great kabbalists. For example, tours take place at locations where kabbalists may have studied or been buried, or where ancient texts like the *Zohar* were authored. International events provide students from all over the world with an opportunity to make connections to unique energy available at certain times of the year. At these events, students meet with other students, share experiences and build friendships.

Volunteering. In the spirit of Kabbalah's principles that emphasize sharing, The Centre provides a volunteer program so that students can participate in charitable initiatives, which includes sharing the wisdom of

Kabbalah itself through a mentoring program. Every year, hundreds of student volunteers organize projects that benefit their communities such as feeding the homeless, cleaning beaches and visiting hospital patients.

One-on-One. The Kabbalah Centre seeks to ensure that each student is supported in his or her study. Teachers and mentors are part of the educational infrastructure that is available to students 24 hours a day, seven days a week.

Hundreds of teachers are available worldwide for students as well as a study program for their continued development. Study takes place in person, by phone, in study groups, through webinars, and even self-directed study in audio format or online.

Mentorship. The Centre's mentor program provides new students with a mentor to help them better understand the kabbalistic principles and teachings. The mentors are experienced Kabbalah students who are interested in supporting new students.

Publishing. Each year, The Centre translates and publishes some of the most challenging kabbalistic texts for advanced scholars including the *Zohar*, *Writings of the Ari*, and the *Ten Luminous Emanations with Commentary*. Drawing from these sources The Kabbalah Centre publishes books yearly in more than 30 languages that are tailored for both beginner- and intermediate-level students and distributed around the world.

***Zohar* Project.** The *Zohar*, the primary text of kabbalistic wisdom, is a commentary on biblical and spiritual matters composed and compiled over 2000 years ago and is believed to be a source of Light. Kabbalists believe that when it is brought into areas of darkness and turmoil, the *Zohar* can create change and bring about improvement. The Kabbalah Centre's *Zohar* Project shares the *Zohar* in 95 countries by distributing free copies to organizations and individuals in recognition of their service to the community and to areas where there is danger. In the past year, over 50,000 copies of the *Zohar* were donated to hospitals, embassies, places of worship, universities, not-for-profit organizations, emergency services, war zones, natural disaster locations, soldiers, pilots, government officials, medical professionals, humanitarian aid workers, and more.

With the merit of this book we would like to awaken love for no reason
in people's hearts towards each other.

With deep appreciation of the work of the Rav and Karen,
may we all always choose the path of living the truth.

With everlasting thanks to the Rav and Karen
for awakening our souls by opening so many eyes and hearts
of the world to the wisdom of Kabbalah.

This book is also dedicated to my mother, in blessed memory,
who first showed me how to love for no reason
and how to always see the good in all people and in every situation.

This book is also dedicated to all of the righteous souls
to come to this world, past, present and future.

We wish to merit this precious gift.